THE RENAISSANCE

English literature in its historical, cultural and social contexts

Patrick Lee-Browne

Facts On File, Inc.

The Renaissance

Facts On File, Inc.
132 West 31st Street
New York NY 10001

Library of Congress Cataloging-in-Publication Data

Backgrounds to English Literature
        p. cm.
    Includes bibliographical references and indexes.
    Contents: v. 1. The Renaissance / Patrick Lee-Browne — v. 2. The romantics / Neil King — v. 3. The Victorians / Aidan Cruttenden — v. 4. The modernist period 1900–1945 / Patrick Lee-Browne — v. 5. Post-war literature 1945 to the present / Caroline Merz and Patrick Lee-Browne
    ISBN 0-8160-5125-9 (set : alk. paper) — ISBN 0-8160-5126-7 (v.1 : alk. paper)
    1. English literature—History and criticism. 2. Literature and history—Great Britain. 3. Great Britain—Civilization.

    PR25 .B33 2002
    820.9—dc21   2002071284

Facts On File books are available at special discounts when purchased in bulk quantities for businesses, associations, institutions, or sales promotions. Please call our Special Sales Department in New York at (212) 967-8800 or (800) 322-8755.

You can find Facts On File on the World Wide Web at http://www.factsonfile.com

Printed in Italy by G. Canale and C. S.p.A. - Turin

10 9 8 7 6 5 4 3 2 1

Editor: Nicola Barber
Consultant: Dr Robert Wilcher, Senior Lecturer in English,
                 University of Birmingham
Design: Simon Borrough
Production: Jenny Mulvanny

Acknowledgments
p.60:   from *Collected Poems 1909-1962* by T.S.Eliot.
             By permission of Faber and Faber Ltd.
Cover: the art archive
p.9:   The Bridgeman Art Library
p.17:   The Bridgeman Art Library
p.27:   The Bridgeman Art Library
p.31:   By courtesy of the National Portrait Gallery
p.35:   the art archive
p.41:   the art archive
p.43:   the art archive
p.49:   Reproduced by permission of the Shakespeare Centre Library
p.57:   (left) Reproduced by permission of the British Library
             (right) The Bridgeman Art Library
p.63:   The Bridgeman Art Library
p.71:   The Bridgeman Art Library
p.81:   The Bridgeman Art Library

First published by Evans Brothers Limited, 2A Portman Mansions, Chiltern Street, London W1U 6NR, United Kingdom

CONTENTS

1. AN AGE OF DISCOVERY

The Renaissance started in Italy in the mid 14th century. The term comes from the French word for 'rebirth', and refers to the revival of ancient Classical Greek and Roman philosophy, literature and art, after much of this learning had been lost during the Middle Ages. The Roman Empire was destroyed in the 5th century (Rome was sacked in AD410) and over the course of time the elaborate social and physical structures that the Romans had established all over Europe decayed, and with them much artistic and cultural activity. The Catholic Church remained as the single unifying force, and it used its power to mold society in both religious and secular spheres. The pope was the supreme authority in all matters in Europe, controlling armies, owning cities and dictating politics in many countries. Kings and princes were subject to his will, which was implemented, theoretically, by the Holy Roman Emperor.

In the course of the 12th and 13th centuries, increasing sophistication of thought and improvements in the quality of individuals' lives led people to challenge the religious dominance of the Church, and to seek alternative sources of authority. The spread of knowledge and learning that accompanied the Renaissance was helped by the development of printing in Europe in the second half of the 15th century. The cultural changes of the Renaissance were closely tied in with the religious, political and economic changes that took place across Europe in the course of the next 300 years, one of the most significant being the call for the reformation of the Catholic Church, which led to the creation of various Protestant churches (see page 6).

The starting point of the Renaissance in England is usually accepted as the accession of Henry VII to the throne after the Battle of Bosworth in 1485. The end of the period is less clear-cut, but is often considered to be marked by the publication of John Milton's *Paradise Lost* in 1667. The high-water mark of the English Renaissance was a period of 15 years or so either side of 1600 which saw the end of the reign of Elizabeth I (reigned 1558-1603) and the beginning of the reign of James I of England and VI of Scotland (reigned 1603-25). William Shakespeare (1564-1616) was only one of many major literary figures who contributed to this remarkable period of literary creativity; others included Christopher Marlowe, Ben Jonson, John Donne, Sir Philip Sidney and Edmund Spenser. After a century of change and upheaval in every aspect of the nation's life, the decade of the 1590s witnessed an astonishing burst of creativity in many aspects of English artistic life, encouraged by Elizabeth herself, who wanted her court to exemplify the finest achievements of European culture. Her reign had already lasted 30 years, and the stability afforded by her careful management of domestic and foreign politics created an atmosphere in which writers, artists and philosophers could prosper, and on which James I would build in the early years of his reign.

Religion

The single most important influence on the English Renaissance was the break with Rome by Henry VIII (reigned 1509-47) and the subsequent establishment of the Protestant Church of England. This occurred in 1534 and set in train the sequence of events known as the English Reformation (see page 6). The Catholic Church had a powerful influence on almost every aspect of life in the Middle Ages, but one of the characteristics of the Renaissance was that this overwhelming influence was challenged: the rediscovery of old authorities and the development of new ways of reflecting on contemporary life was driven not only by the Church but also by independent-minded scholars and intellectuals. A central belief of the Catholic Church was that mankind was inherently sinful as a result of the 'Original Sin' of Adam and Eve in the Garden of Eden, and that the purpose of each individual's life was to make amends by doing 'good works' for the sin that they had inherited by virtue of being born. Protestants also believed in Original Sin, but maintained that salvation could not be earned, but was the free gift of God, attainable 'by faith alone'. The study of Classical texts, coupled with developments in scientific research, led to a more objective assessment of Catholic beliefs, and correspondingly to various challenges to established Christian practice and thinking. Although the effects were slow and piecemeal, the influence of Renaissance figures such as Desiderius Erasmus, Niccolò Machiavelli, Nicolaus Copernicus and Galileo Galilei profoundly altered people's perceptions of their relationship with God and nature, and of the nature of the universe itself.

Renaissance humanism

The way of thinking that was retrospectively termed 'Renaissance humanism' recognized the potential in mankind and celebrated human achievement. It was a reaction to the negative, guilt-laden view of 'fallen' man encouraged by the Church. The humanist movement began with the re-evaluation of Classical texts: the Church had appropriated many of these texts for its own purposes, but Renaissance scholars approached them free from fixed theological positions and used them to illustrate the civilizing power of the Classics. In particular, they aimed to demonstrate the value of rational or 'scientific' thinking over instinctive belief, and to show that secular values (ways of thinking that did not start from

Scripture or theology) could be as valid as Christian ones. The main humanist thinkers were themselves Christians, but not afraid to use their ideas to challenge the official line of the Catholic Church. Desiderius Erasmus (1469-1536) was a Dutch scholar whose influence spread into theological debates in all the major countries of Europe. He based his scholarship on close re-reading of the Greek New Testament and the authorities of the early Church, but his criticism of the abuses of the contemporary Church and the independence of his views meant that he was viewed with suspicion by conventional theologians. Although his work and views coincided with Martin Luther's challenge to the Church (see below), he distanced himself from Luther and the Protestant movement, preferring to pursue his own line of inquiry.

The Reformation

The Reformation in Europe was a large-scale protest against the Catholic Church inspired by political developments (countries such as the Netherlands and various German states wanted to be free from Italian or Spanish control); by moral considerations (the Church was seen to be corrupt and badly served by its clergy); and by disagreement about fundamental areas of Christian belief. The challenge to the Roman Catholic Church was led by a German monk, Martin Luther (1483-1546), who famously nailed an attack on the sale of indulgences (a form of pardon for sins already committed) to the door of the Castle Church in Wittenberg in 1517. Luther's challenge – on the teachings as well as the practices of the Catholic Church – started a groundswell of dissent in Northern Europe which led eventually to the emergence of the Protestant churches. Another major figure in the Reformation in Europe was the Frenchman Jean Calvin (1509-64), who advocated a very strict moral code of behaviour; he lived for much of his life in Geneva, where the emphasis on civic responsibility and religious observance meant that his views on drinking, sex, public entertainment and swearing were encoded in the local laws. His followers in France were known as Huguenots.

— SIR THOMAS MORE —

Erasmus's best known work, In Praise of Folly *(1511) was written at the house of another of the major humanists, Sir Thomas More (1477-1535). More was a lawyer who rose through local government in London to become the Lord Chancellor to Henry VIII, the highest office in the state. However, he became involved in the religious and political wrangling over Henry's marriage to his first wife, Catherine of Aragon (see page 7). As a result of his refusal to recognize Henry's marriage to Anne Boleyn, because it denied the supremacy of the pope over the Church in England, More was executed. During his lifetime, More combined scholarship with his political career: he wrote a highly influential* History of King Richard III *(c.1513-18), but he is best known for his book, written in Latin,* Utopia *(1516). The name was coined by More, from the Greek ou-topos ('no place') as a pun on eu-topos ('place where all is well'). Among the features of More's Utopian state were a lack of private property, free state education, tolerance of all religions, divorce, euthanasia and women's rights. In its celebration of human happiness through personal and collective fulfillment, it typifies the spirit of Renaissance humanism.*

The English Reformation

Just as England enjoyed its own Renaissance, so too it experienced
its own version of the Reformation. The first phase of the
Reformation in England was a political one: Henry VIII, who in his
early years was a keen persecutor of anti-Catholic activists and was
rewarded with the title of 'Defender of the Faith' by the pope,
married Catherine of Aragon in 1509. Catherine gave birth to five
children, but only one survived – Mary. Henry wanted a son, so he
started to look for an excuse to divorce Catherine in order to marry
his mistress Anne Boleyn. The matter was referred to the pope who
was unable, for diplomatic reasons, to grant a divorce.
Nevertheless, Henry married Anne Boleyn in 1533. The following
year he passed acts declaring that the pope had no authority in
England and making himself head of the English Church.

Henry used the split with the Roman Catholic Church as an
opportunity to break the social and economic power of the Church
and seize its wealth to further his own political ends. He confiscated
the valuable assets accumulated over many centuries by the
monasteries and abbeys both in centers of population and in the
country at large. In some places, buildings were destroyed or given
to Henry's favorites and followers for domestic use; in others
schools and cathedrals were founded on the sites. This process,
known as the Dissolution of the Monasteries, was carried out by
Henry's minister, Thomas Cromwell, between 1536 and 1539.

The second phase of the English Reformation took place after
Henry's death, during the reigns of his son Edward VI and elder
daughter Mary. Edward VI (reigned 1547-53) was only ten when
Henry died, and England was ruled by two regents, first the Duke of
Somerset and then the Duke of Northumberland. Both men, with
the approval of the young but intellectually advanced Edward, took
the country further towards Protestantism. They carried out various
measures including the right of the clergy to marry (Catholic priests
were required to remain single) and the publication of *The Book of
Common Prayer* in 1549, which provided for all forms of worship
(the 'liturgy') to be conducted in English for the first time (see page
52). Edward died of tuberculosis at the age of 15, and in the last
year of his life he worked with Northumberland to prevent either of
his sisters Mary or Elizabeth from succeeding him, fearful that they
would take England back to Catholicism. As a result, Lady Jane
Grey, the daughter-in-law of Northumberland, succeeded Edward as
a puppet monarch for nine days (10-19 July 1553) before being
overthrown by a popular revolt that put Mary on the throne to which
she was entitled.

Mary I (reigned 1553-8) indeed did all she could to undo the
English Reformation: despite popular feeling in the country she

married Philip II of Spain, restored the Catholic liturgy (which was conducted in Latin) and imposed harsh laws against non-believers. In 1554 she successfully thwarted a revolt by Sir Thomas Wyatt (son of the poet, see page 67) by appealing to her subjects' loyalty, but the remaining four years of her reign were marked by the vicious punishment and execution of heretics, an unsuccessful war against France, and personal disappointment in childlessness, illness and in the realization that the majority of the population feared and hated her.

Mary was succeeded by her sister Elizabeth, who trod carefully between the competing claims of Catholics and Protestants. By the Acts of Supremacy and Uniformity (1559) she restored the Protestant faith, together with many of the earlier reforms contained in the English Prayer Book and the articles of faith, which defined the central beliefs of the Church of England. But Elizabeth created a state of relative religious tolerance by removing Catholics from positions of power while rejecting the attempts of the more radical reformers, known as Puritans, to bring England into line with Continental Protestantism. Elizabeth had survived years of imprisonment and the threat of execution by maintaining a diplomatic advantage over her adversaries, and she used her experience to the benefit of the country by rejecting extremism of any kind. The consequence of this benign tolerance was a widespread respect and admiration for her that manifested itself in the cultural blossoming of the 1590s.

Science

The universe

The challenge to the authority of the Catholic Church in Renaissance Europe was complimented and fostered by corresponding developments in the sciences. Medieval and early Renaissance understanding of the natural world was heavily influenced by the writing of two Greek philosophers, Aristotle (384-322BC) and Plato (c.428-348BC). Aristotle's political and scientific thinking was based on the idea that the world operated on a system of logical and universal laws. Medieval thought linked this rational view of the universe to the theory developed by the Egyptian astronomer and geographer Ptolemy (c.90-168). In Ptolemy's model the Earth was at the center of a series of concentric spheres carrying each of the known planets (Mars, Mercury, Venus, Jupiter, Saturn), the Moon, the Sun and the fixed stars. The movement of the heavenly bodies within their orbits was believed to create a kind of harmonic vibration known as the 'music of the spheres', inaudible to humans because of their sinful mortality.

The essence of Plato's writing was that the material, familiar

George Gower (attr.),
***Elizabeth I* (the Armada Portrait), (c.1588)**
This painting, commemorating the destruction of the Spanish Armada
in 1588, is typical of the Renaissance use of iconography (aspects of a
painting that have a particular significance because of their context) to
give extra significance to art. The arrival and destruction of the Armada
are shown in two windows, in the center of which sits Elizabeth, her
imperial authority signified by the diadem and by the globe that rests
under her right hand. There is no unifying perspective to the portrait –
each element has its own geometry – but the message is clear:
Elizabeth has triumphed over the foreign threat to her kingdom and she
remains queen of a global empire.

world around us is a projection, an imperfect imitation, of an eternal world of ideal forms beyond the reach of our senses. Plato used the analogy of a group of people in a cave to put across his idea: they can see shadows moving across the wall of the cave, and so know that something is making the shadows, but they cannot see the reality that casts the shadows. The metaphysical awareness of a spiritual force in the universe in Platonism was matched by Aristotle's use of observation to assume the existence of a supreme logic at work in the universe. The theories of both these philosophers and the ordered, Earth-centered view of the universe of Ptolemy were used by the Church to reinforce its idea of a structured and hierarchical Christian creation.

This medieval world picture was upset by the work of the 16th-century astronomers, whose discoveries led to a complete rethinking of the structure of the universe. In 1543, Nicolaus Copernicus (1473-1543) published *On the Revolutions of the Celestial Spheres*, which suggested that the Sun, rather than the Earth, was at the center of the universe, and that the universe was much larger than had previously been thought. Copernicus's work was followed up by other astronomers, the most notable of whom were Tycho Brahe (1546-1601), Johannes Kepler (1571-1630) and Galileo Galilei (1564-1642). But it was not until his invention of the telescope in around 1608 – allowing detailed observation of the heavens – that Galileo could prove Copernicus's theory to be correct. Until then it had been treated as an unproven hypothesis and so not considered as a real threat by the Church. But when the Church leaders realized that part of the fabric of their Christian teaching was threatened by Copernican theory, they conspired with the papal authorities to have Galileo's work suspended, and Copernican theory declared 'false and erroneous'. From then until his death, Galileo remained in conflict with the Church, suffering house arrest for the last eight years of his life.

The reason why the astronomical revolution was a threat to the Church was because it offered a demonstrably powerful alternative – scientific, rational deduction – to faith and theological scholarship. It also undermined the fundamentalist approach to Scripture (a belief in a literal interpretation of the Bible), because the Earth and mankind were no longer at the centre of the universe that God had created. The ability to create the tools to probe into the unknown, such as the telescope or the microscope, was seen as further evidence of human achievement, rather than a divine gift, fueling the development of the humanist approach to progress.

Humours

From the Middle Ages to the Renaissance many people believed that there was a correspondence between the workings of the cosmos and the activity of human society, and also between society at large (the 'body politic') and the individual human body. In this way, social or political disorder such as rebellion or killing the king would be reflected by similar disorder in the heavens – the presence of comets, eclipses, violent or unpredictable weather or other unnatural events. For example, in Shakespeare's *King Lear*, (c.1605) the Earl of Gloucester says:

> 'These late eclipses in the sun and moon portend no good to us. Though the wisdom of nature can reason it thus and thus, yet nature finds itself scourged by the sequent effects. Love cools, friendship falls off, brothers divide; in cities, mutinies; in countries, discord; in palaces, treason; and the bond cracked 'twixt son and father.'

A similar relationship was understood to exist between the make-up of the natural world and of the human body. One branch of Aristotelian science that survived into the literature of the 17th century was the theory of humours. This maintained that the four elements – earth, water, air and fire – and the four seasons of the year were reflected in the four humours (liquids) that were thought to make up the human form: black bile (melancholy), phlegm, blood (sanguine) and yellow bile (choler). In an ideal world these four humours would be equally balanced, but, on the whole, a person's character would be the result of the predominance of one or more humours. So someone who had more than his fair share of black bile would be naturally inclined to be melancholic, while someone with an imbalance of phlegm would be lethargic or sluggish. By the end of the 16th century the word

—— MELANCHOLY ——

In 1621, the scholar Robert Burton (1577-1640) published a comprehensive compendium of medical and scientific learning entitled The Anatomy of Melancholy. *Melancholy (supposedly caused by an excess of black bile) was considered the worst and hardest to overcome of the humours, because it fed upon itself and could lead to melancholy madness. Burton describes some of the attributes of melancholy as follows:*

'Suspicion and jealousy are general symptoms: they are commonly distrustful, timorous, apt to mistake and amplify, facile irascibiles [easily angered], testy, peevish and ready to snarl upon every small occasion... Now prodigal, and then covetous, they do, and by-and-by repent them of that which they have done, so that both ways they are troubled, whether they do or not do, want [lack] or have, hit or miss...'

The state of melancholy had become a fashionable interest in the 1590s. The 'melancholy man', often a lover, a poet or a satirist, had appeared on the stage in The Merchant of Venice *(Antonio),* As You Like It *(Jaques) and Jonson's* Every Man in his Humour *(the two poetasters). The character of Hamlet in Shakespeare's play is the most complex example, although sometimes his melancholy is affected, sometimes genuine. Speaking to his former friends Rosencrantz and Guildenstern, Hamlet declares:*

'I have of late, but wherefore I know not, lost all my mirth, forgone all custom of exercises; and indeed it goes so heavily with my disposition that this goodly frame, the earth, seems to me a sterile promontory; this most excellent canopy the air, look you, this brave o'erhanging firmament, this majestical roof fretted with golden fire — why, it appeareth no other thing to me but a foul and pestilent collection of vapours.'

———————

'humours' came to include the sense of someone having an obsession or doing things on a whim. The playwright Ben Jonson (1572-1637) turned the notion of the humours to dramatic advantage; he associated humours with the distortion of human nature by greed or vanity. As he stated in the Induction (preface) to *Every Man out of his Humour:*

> 'when some one peculiar quality
> Doth so possess a man, that it doth draw
> All his affects, his spirits, and his powers
> In their confluctions, all to run one way,
> This may be truly said to be, a Humour.'

Many of the characters in his plays, such as Sir Politic Would-Be in *Volpone* (1605), Sir Epicure Mammon in *The Alchemist* (1610) or Fitzdotterel in *The Devil is an Ass* (1616), expose themselves to exploitation by thieves and confidence tricksters and are brought to judgment as a result of allowing their humours to get the better of them. In the prologue to *The Alchemist* Jonson writes:

> 'Our scene is London, 'cause we would make known
> No country's mirth is better than our own.
> No clime breeds better matter, for your whore,
> Bawd, squire, impostor, many persons more,
> Whose manners, now call'd humours, feed the stage.'

Medicine

Medical science was slow to develop during the Renaissance, reliant as it was on the principle of the humours. Treatment for illnesses had the objective of restoring balance to the body, either by bleeding the patient, delivering purgatives, or adminstering herbal remedies. The only alternative, when things became serious, was to carry out unsophisticated surgical operations without anaesthetic or sterilisation of the instruments. Surgery was generally not undertaken by doctors but by barbers, but during the 16th century medicine and surgery grew closer together. Anatomy was an important branch of medical training, and a significant breakthrough came with the discovery of the circulation of the blood by William Harvey (1578-1657). Aristotelian science held that the blood vessels contained both blood and air. The Greco-Roman physician Galen, in the 2nd century AD proved that the arteries contained only blood but it was believed that the heart was supplied with air to the right side from the lungs. It was also understood that the movement of the blood was by ebb and flow, an analogy being found in the movement of the sea. Harvey learned much while training as an anatomist at the University of Padua in Italy, and spent the early decades of the 17th century in observation and experimentation, enjoying the patronage of both James I and Charles I. In 1628 he finally published his theory in a book entitled *An Anatomical Exercise Concerning the Motion of the Heart and Blood in Animals*. In it he established the true nature of the circulation of the blood, although his theory provoked widespread controversy, and it was many years before it was proved beyond doubt to be correct and widely accepted.

Exploration

The age of European expeditions to the Americas began partly as a result of the desire to find a westward sea route to the Far East. For centuries the spice trade with Cathay (China) had been highly lucrative but had been limited by the difficult and slow travelling involved. The expedition of Christopher Columbus in 1492, which resulted in his landfall in the Caribbean, was the first of many attempts to find a sea route to the East. The early exploratory voyages from Europe to the New World and elsewhere were mostly carried out by Italians with backing from the courts of Spain and Portugal: Columbus himself; Vasco da Gama, who sailed round the Cape of Good Hope to East Africa and India in 1497-9; Amerigo Vespucci and Pedro Cabral, who reached Brazil in separate voyages from 1499 to 1500; Vasco Balboa, who crossed the Isthmus of Panama in 1513 to be the first European to reach the Pacific Ocean. The one early English venture was by John Cabot, actually Genoese by birth, who was supported by Henry VII in his journey in 1497, looking for the elusive Northwest Passage that would take him through to the Far East.

Once the vast wealth of the Americas had been discovered, the emphasis changed from navigation to exploitation and *conquistadors* (conquerors), such as Hernando Cortés and Francisco Pizarro, moved into the interior of Central and South America to seize the vast wealth of the Aztec and Inca empires. By the mid-16th century Spain had already established a substantial empire in the New World, and was able to use the great mineral resources there to fund its European armies and fleets. This process was helped by the division of the spoils of the Americas between Spain and Portugal at the Treaty of Tordesillas in 1494, arranged by Pope Alexander VI. The treaty divided the New World into Portuguese and Spanish zones and gave the Spanish monarchs, Isabella and Ferdinand, control over the Church in the lands they colonized.

The realization of the possibilities that lay across the Atlantic Ocean took longer to reach England, partly because there was a well-established and profitable wool trade with Flanders which delayed the need to find new markets and sources of wealth. In 1553, Richard

Chancellor travelled eastwards in search of a northeast passage to China, ending up in the White Sea and establishing trade links with Russia instead. However, it was only from the 1570s onwards that English navigators started sailing westwards. In the 1570s and '80s Sir Martin Frobisher and Sir Humphrey Gilbert both made attempts to establish colonies on the northeast coast of America, though with little success. But the Elizabethan venturers who preferred to fight the Spanish for their gold achieved a more lasting fame. Queen Elizabeth sanctioned piracy against Spanish treasure ships by granting privateering licences to individuals to attack enemy shipping on behalf of the Crown, and keep any spoils for themselves.

Sir Francis Drake (c.1540-96) was involved in several privateering voyages to the West Indies, but it was his circumnavigation of the world in 1577-80 which really made his name: he was knighted on the deck of his ship, the *Golden Hind,* by Elizabeth on his return. Drake's subsequent exploits in the West Indies did great damage to the Spanish economy, while his leading role in the defeat of the Armada in 1588 sealed a career which relied on verve and opportunism as much as on skill and application.

Sir Walter Raleigh (1552-1618) was a similarly mercurial character. He is credited with the founding of the colony of Virginia (present-day North Carolina), although he never personally set foot there; he led an expedition up the Orinoco River in present-day Guiana in search of the mythical city of Eldorado; he was involved in a raid on Cadiz in 1596 which was organized by the Earl of Essex. As one of Queen Elizabeth's favorites, he enjoyed considerable political and financial status, and was granted large estates in Ireland (then an English colony, see page 15). When James I came to the throne, however, Raleigh found himself out of favor: James was keen to make peace with Spain, but Raleigh was against any treaty with England's traditional enemy. In 1603 Raleigh was accused of treason on a trumped-up charge of being involved in a Spanish plot against the king and imprisoned in the Tower of London. He was released from prison, with the king's permission, in 1616 to mount another expedition to Guiana in order to bring back the gold he was convinced was there. The venture went badly wrong: once at the mouth of the Orinoco, Raleigh suffered a fever which limited his involvement in the ensuing action. His lieutenant attacked a Spanish settlement, and Raleigh's son was killed in the action. The expedition returned empty-handed. King James was not impressed, and Raleigh was executed.

Drake and Raleigh are only two of the many famous seamen who spread England's maritime influence abroad. Sir John Hawkins, Sir Richard Grenville and Thomas Howard, Earl of Suffolk also sailed and fought for queen and country. However, their activity was not altogether laudable. During Elizabeth's reign, for example, Portugal alone was licensed to conduct the trade of slaves from its West African colonies to the West Indies and Brazil. Sir John Hawkins chose to set up his own slave-trading business from Guinea to the Spanish West Indies in 1562-3, provoking a diplomatic row with Spain. Elizabeth denounced Hawkins's activities in public while granting him a coat of arms, lending him ships and giving him other financial support in private. The slave trade, deemed necessary because the indigenous populations of the Caribbean and Brazil had been decimated by diseases imported from Europe and by ill-treatment at the hands of their conquerors, continued from ports such as Bristol and Liverpool until its abolition at the beginning of the 19th century.

Ireland

Though geographically close, Ireland and the Irish were considered by the English to be almost as alien and savage as the land and people of the New World. Many of the men who had travelled unsuccessfully across the Atlantic in search of new territories (Sir Martin Frobisher, Sir Walter Raleigh and Sir Humphrey Gilbert, for example) annexed large tracts of land, known as 'plantations', in Ireland. The country had been invaded by the English in earlier centuries, but Elizabethan settlement was more systematic, and made more of a concerted attempt to subjugate the country to English law and religious practice. Disputes arose between the old Anglo-Irish nobles, who had in many cases bred into the Irish ruling classes, and the new ones. Successive Governor-Generals, including the father of Sir Philip Sidney (see page 61), failed to suppress Irish resistance; Edmund Spenser served as secretary to another Governor-General, Lord Grey, and wrote about the conflicts and issues of Irish colonization in Book V of *The Faerie Queene* (see page 68).

In 1598 the Earl of Tyrone, an Ulster nobleman, led an uprising against English rule. Spenser and other 'planters' were forced to flee back to England after their houses were looted and burned down. Elizabeth sent the Earl of Essex to put down the revolt, but without success; Essex was replaced by the Earl of Mountjoy, who finally defeated Tyrone a few days after Elizabeth's death in March 1603. The English victory marked the first real imposition of control in Ireland since the days of Henry II (reigned 1154-89) and made way for the first successful plantations in Northern Ireland during James I's reign. However, progress towards a peaceful settlement of the country was prevented by the simultaneous movement of dissident Scots Presbyterians into the northeast of Ulster, who took land from the defeated Irish, but stuck rigidly to their Protestant faith and cultural identity rather than finding common ground with the community into which they had settled.

The Tudor court

The Wars of the Roses was a long drawn-out struggle for power between the two rival branches of the House of Plantaganet, York and Lancaster, after the death of Henry V in 1422. The reigns of his son Henry VI, and then Edward IV, Edward V and Richard III were dominated by attempts from both sides to take and secure the throne. Henry Tudor, a member of the house of Lancaster, was crowned Henry VII after his defeat of Richard III at the Battle of Bosworth in 1485. He followed up his victory by marrying Elizabeth of York, the daughter of Edward IV, in order to unite the two families. In this way, Henry VII established the Tudor dynasty as a strong and stabilizing one after the destructive feuding of the Wars of the Roses.

Under the Tudor monarchs the royal court developed not only as the center of political activity for the whole country, but also as the cultural center. The tradition of royal patronage was, of course, not new, but the Tudor monarchs – in particular Henry VIII and Elizabeth I – used it to strengthen their control over their nobles. By the beginning of the 16th century the court had changed from being simply the private household of the monarch to being the center of a body of advisors concerned with the administrative government of the country. Importantly, the court was mostly based in London, rather than following the monarch around the country. The Privy Chamber, later called the Privy Council, was the inner core of advisors who were entrusted with the highest respon-sibilities and secrets of the state: men such as Thomas Cromwell and Sir Thomas More under Henry VIII and Sir Francis Walsingham, William Cecil (Lord Burghley) and his son Robert Cecil (Earl of Salisbury) under Elizabeth. The hierarchical structure of the court and the attraction towards the center of power that it created led to infighting and factions, but that

—— WILLIAM CAXTON ——

By 1485 the influence of the European Renaissance was already making itself felt in England, helped and typified by the work of William Caxton (c.1422-c.91). After a career in the wool trade with Flanders, Caxton turned his attentions to the translation, and then printing, of French literature. He printed the first book in English, The Recuyell of the Historyes of Troye *in Bruges in 1475, and developed a successful business at his press in Westminster when he returned to England at the end of 1476. In the course of the next 15 years he published much of the English literature available, including Geoffrey Chaucer's* The Canterbury Tales, *John Gower's* Confessio Amantis, *the poetry of John Lydgate and, in 1485, Sir Thomas Malory's* Morte Darthur. *This last work provides a symbolic bridge between the feudal and early modern worlds. Written in prose in what is now referred to as Middle English — the language in which* The Canterbury Tales, The Vision of Piers Plowman *and* Sir Gawain and the Green Knight *were all written —* Morte Darthur *tells the story of King Arthur and the Knights of the Round Table. It draws on earlier French verse romances but emphasizes instances of brotherhood and fellowship rather than the courtly love and individual acts of nobility which characterize its sources. In its subject matter it evokes the feudal world of the medieval period in which Malory was still writing, but as one of the earliest printed books in English it marks the start of a new age in which, slowly but steadily, the process of standardization began, as a result of which London and the southeast were confirmed as the center of cultural and political life in England.*

Hans Holbein the Younger, *The Ambassadors* (1533)

The two men are Jean de Dinteville and Georges de Selve, French envoys at the court of Henry VIII. The wealth of objects associated with Renaissance humanism is counterpoised with the anamorphic painting (painted with a distorted perspective) of a skull in the foreground. See page 18 for more discussion of the painting.

same friction was responsible for much of the literary and artistic creation of the 16th century, whether satirizing the court and its practices or celebrating its members and their achievements.

The painting *The Ambassadors* (see illustration page 17) by Hans Holbein the Younger (1497-1543), court painter to Henry VIII, illustrates how both facets – endorsing the values of the court and simultaneously presenting an alternative interpretation – could be combined in one work of art. The painting, which hangs in the National Gallery in London, represents Jean de Dinteville and Georges de Selve, two ambassadors of Francis I of France at the court of Henry VIII. The men are shown at ease in the midst of objects of Renaissance culture: a lute, celestial and terrestrial globes, mathematical and astronomical instruments and various theological texts. But slashing across the foot of the painting is a blur that can only be interpreted when viewed from the right angle, almost level with the plane of the canvas. The blur turns out to be a skull, a reminder of human mortality and the vanity of human efforts to achieve glory. Almost concealed behind the drapery on the left of the picture is a crucifix: religion sidelined by the extravagance of worldly life. Other details such as the setting of the painting – the chapel in Westminster Abbey where the pregnant Anne Boleyn was hurriedly crowned queen to reinforce the legitimacy as an heir to the throne of the child that was born a few months later – the choice of texts, and the broken string on the lute all reinforce a less optimistic note in the painting that runs counter to its surface 'meaning'.

Holbein's painting contains all the essential ingredients of the English Renaissance: the pervasive influence of religion; the interplay of state and church politics; the achievements of the European Renaissance and the influence of humanism on education and culture. But above all it reminds us of the autonomy of the artist: his freedom to take decisions about how to depict the people and situations with which he was presented and to provoke informed discussion about how to interpret his work.

2 . D R A M A

There was an unbroken tradition of drama from the medieval period to the theatrical world in which Christopher Marlowe, William Shakespeare and Ben Jonson worked, but in the course of the 16th century – and particularly in the last three decades – the kinds of plays being performed and the conditions in which the performances took place changed dramatically. For example, when a permanent stage was established at the Red Lion at Whitechapel in 1567 it was the first structure built for the purpose of presenting plays to the public. Yet, within 30 years or so the well-known playhouses on the south bank of the River Thames such as the Rose, the Globe, the Swan and the Fortune, and others on the outskirts of the City of London such as the Theatre in Shoreditch and the Blackfriars theatre, had all been built.

Public drama

Public drama in the medieval period was mostly religious in its subject matter and in the circumstances in which it was acted. It was not a year-round entertainment; rather, it was a way of celebrating the holy days that marked the major festivals of the religious calendar, in particular Christmas and Epiphany, Shrovetide, Whitsun (or Pentecost) and Corpus Christi. On these occasions, drama was an integral part of the feasting, drinking and sense of community. So although the scripts were concerned with religious or moral subjects, they were often full of humor, oaths and swearing, popular clichés and real-life situations. The anonymous authors of medieval dramas were obviously concerned to communicate a moral message based on the teachings of Christianity, but they knew their audience and the conditions in which their plays were performed, and strong characterization and vivid scenes played an important part in putting the moral issues into a realistic and familiar context.

An English translation of the Bible was not printed until the 1530s and church services were conducted in Latin until the introduction of *The Book of Common Prayer* in 1549 (revised in 1552 and again in 1559 after the Catholic interregnum of Mary, see page 7). So-called 'mystery' or 'miracle' plays (see Glossary of Terms) were therefore an important means of teaching the Old Testament stories and the message of the gospels to ordinary people, as well as presenting theological issues such as the conflict between worldly and religious authority and the means of salvation.

There was a close link between the Church and civic authorities, and this is perhaps seen most clearly in the strong tradition of plays written in a number of towns and cities across the country to celebrate the feast of Corpus Christi. Manuscripts have survived of virtually complete cycles of mystery plays re-telling episodes from the Bible from the Creation to the Last Judgement, written for the festivities at York, Chester, Wakefield and, probably, Bury St Edmunds. Other individual plays have survived from places such as Coventry, Newcastle-upon-Tyne and Norwich. The evidence makes it clear that the various city guilds each took responsibility for particular episodes, which were performed on large open carts called 'pageants'. These carts were pulled through the streets along a fixed processional route. At various prescribed stations along the route the cart would stop and the play be acted out. Each individual scene would, therefore, be enacted several times in the course of the day. The whole cycle would often start as early as 4.30 a.m. in order to make sure that the sequence of plays could be completed. It is perhaps no coincidence that the feast of Corpus Christi was chosen for this occasion, since it falls between mid-May and mid-June, when the days are long. In York, there were 12 separate stations along the route, so the city centre would have been alive with simultaneous performances of the various Bible stories. However, the logistics were not always very smooth-running and so at Chester, for example, the mystery cycle was spread over three days in order to simplify proceedings. The influence of the Church throughout the whole community was perhaps no more clearly seen than on such occasions, when the Church and civic authorities paraded and celebrated together.

It was Henry VIII's falling out with the pope (see page 7) that began the demise of the mystery plays. The austere, sober approach of the new Protestant faith meant that the street plays and religious processions associated with Corpus Christi were no longer considered suitable. Moreover, as part of their popular appeal, the mystery plays had always included a fair amount of general political commentary on the danger of kings and princes who set themselves up as rivals to God's authority – something Henry VIII was naturally keen to suppress. In fact, the Tudors – from Henry VII through to Elizabeth I – were notable for their concern to control the Church and the other institutions of state through propaganda, coercion and other political means. Public drama offered many opportunities for anti-authoritarian sentiments to be expressed, and was therefore viewed with considerable suspicion. In 1548 it was made illegal to celebrate the feast of Corpus Christi, and by the 1580s the mystery plays had ceased to be performed.

Indoor performance

Although the popular image of medieval drama is one of open-air pageants, dramatic performances also took place indoors in the great halls of the houses of the aristocracy, in town and city guildhalls, in the colleges of Oxford and Cambridge universities, and in the Inns of Court. Plays for privileged, intellectual audiences were often written in Latin, whereas those for public performance were invariably written in the common tongue – English.

This other side to drama – that of indoor performance – was equally important in the evolution of Elizabethan theatre. The Corpus Christi cycles were religious and moralistic, as was another kind of public drama, known as 'morality' plays. These were not based on Biblical scenes as the mystery plays were, but dramatized social and moral issues in a freer form. Plays written for private performance, on the other hand, were often of a non-religious nature, and were written more for entertainment than instruction. An early example of a secular play that nevertheless sits firmly in the tradition of the morality plays is *Magnificence*. This was written between 1516 and 1519 by John Skelton (c.1460-1529), the court poet – the Poet Laureate of his day – of Henry VIII. It was probably performed in the hall of one of the London guilds or livery companies as an entertainment to accompany a large feast or banquet – there are various references to the closeness of the audience and the eating and drinking going on around the action of the play. The play was partly a morality play in the tradition of the 15th-century plays *Everyman* or *The Castle of Perseverance*, but it was also meant as a satirical attack on either Cardinal Wolsey, Chancellor to Henry VIII, or on Henry himself. Wolsey certainly took the play to be aimed at him, but its allegorical (symbolic) treatment of the dangers of corrupt government and of the influence of characters such as Folly and Fancy make it equally likely that Skelton was writing about the royal court in general. The didactic (instructional) nature of the drama of the time is apparent in the ending of the play, when the ruler, Magnificence, is rescued from suicide by characters such as Good Hope, Redress and Perseverance:

'**Magnificence**   Shall I myself hang with a halter? Nay;
                Nay, rather will I choose to rid me of this life
                In sticking myself with this fair knife.

Here Magnificence would slay himself with a knife.

Mischief   Alarum, alarum, too long we abide!
Despair   Out, harrow, hell burneth! Where shall I me
                hide?

Here enters Good Hope, while Despair and Mischief are running away. Let Good Hope suddenly snatch the sword from him and say:

Good Hope	Alas, dear son, sore cumbered is thy mind, Thyself that thou would slo [kill] against nature and kind.
Magnificence	Ah, blessed may ye be, sire. What shall I you call?

Good Hope	Good Hope, sir, my name is; remedy
	    principal
	Against all faults of your ghostly foe.
	Who knoweth me himself may never slo…
	Undoubted ye had lost yourself eternally;
	There is no man may sin more mortally
	Than of wanhope [despair] through the
	    unhappy ways
	By mischief to breviate and shorten his days.'

Acting was encouraged at the Inns of Court, where lawyers trained and worked, because it complemented the skills of oratory and oral performance. It was also cultivated in the universities and grammar schools because it developed the debating and language skills of the students. At that time boys attended the universities of Oxford or Cambridge at any age from 12 to 17, and the subject matter and style of the plays that have survived reflect the relative youthfulness of their audience.

The earliest plays that might be said to belong to the English Renaissance date from the midpoint of the 16th century, during the reigns of Mary and then Elizabeth. The fashion arose for entertainments to be put on during seasonal feasting, and these plays, usually comic and diverting in their subject matter, became known as 'interludes', from the custom of playing them between courses at a feast. Nicholas Udall (1505-56), a schoolmaster and translator as well as playwright, wrote *Ralph Roister Doister* around 1552, possibly to be performed by some of his pupils as a Christmas entertainment. The play draws on a number of different scholarly styles and sources, and owes its plot structure to the Latin comedy of the Roman dramatists Terence and Plautus, but it also contains plenty of knockabout country farce. A similar kind of play, *Gammer Gurton's Needle*, was written by an unknown author to be performed at Christ's College, Cambridge in 1566, and is a bawdy comedy set in a village somewhere in the north of England.

Playwrights at institutions such as the Inns of Court, stately houses or Oxford and Cambridge colleges were usually involved in the production of their own plays, and the actors were usually members of the community. All of these venues had at their center a large hall, often with a dais at one end where the high table sat.

This was used for raised seating for the important spectators. At the other end of the hall there was often a passage running across the building screened off by wooden panels, with a gallery above. The performance would take place on the floor of the hall in front of the screens, allowing the actors to use the passage as a 'backstage' area, while the gallery provided an upper level for acting or for musicians to play from, if appropriate (see the illustration of Penshurst Place on page 81).

Most indoor performances were 'occasional', meaning that they were put on to celebrate a particular event in the life of the family, court or college such as religious feasts, weddings or visits by notable people. The concept of putting on a private performance 'for the sake of it' did not really exist. References to such occasions within a play itself have sometimes been useful in helping to date the composition or first performances of plays. For example, evidence from within the play and from other sources suggests that Shakespeare's *A Midsummer Night's Dream* may have been written to celebrate the wedding of Elizabeth Carey and Thomas Berkeley on 19 February 1596 at the mansion of Sir George Carey in Blackfriars. Sir George and his father were both patrons of Shakespeare's theatre company, the Chamberlain's Men. Evidence in *The Merry Wives of Windsor* indicates that Shakespeare wrote this play for performance at the palace of Whitehall to mark the occasion of the annual Garter ceremony of 23 April 1597, when Sir George was elected as one of the Knights of the Garter. However, in both instances, there is not enough firm evidence to be certain.

—— TWELFTH NIGHT ——

The period between Christmas (25 December) and Twelfth Night (6 January, the eve of the feast of Epiphany) was a time of celebration when the usual rules in institutions no longer applied. Different customs were observed in various places. In English cathedrals, for example, one of the choristers was elected 'boy bishop' for the feast day of St Nicholas (6 December) and took control of the cathedral and its offices for that day. On the continent the same custom was observed on 28 December, the feast day of the Holy Innocents. At the royal court, the Inns of Court and at many Oxford and Cambridge colleges, a 'Lord of Misrule' was elected to oversee the festivities of the 12 days of Christmas. The Lord of Misrule presided over a mock court and everyone in the household was expected to pay due respect to him, regardless of their usual position, and his. The office was abolished at the royal court by Elizabeth when she came to throne – she was also responsible for the abolition of the custom of boy bishops – but the memory of it survived in Renaissance drama. One example is in Shakespeare's Twelfth Night *(c.1600), where the misrule and topsy-turvy that Sir Toby Belch brings to Olivia's court evokes the spirit of Christmas celebrations. Another example can be found in* Henry IV Part I *(c.1597), when Falstaff and Prince Hal are playing the parts of Hal and his father Henry IV in a tavern. Hal, sitting on a mock throne, likens Falstaff to a figure from the old morality drama, and recalls at the same time the image of the Lord of Misrule:*

HAL *Why dost thou converse with… that reverend Vice, that grey Iniquity, that father Ruffian, that Vanity in Years? Wherein is he good, but to taste sack and drink it? Wherein neat and cleanly, but to carve a capon and eat it? Wherein cunning, but in craft? Wherein crafty, but in villainy? Wherein villainous, but in all things? Wherein worthy, but in nothing?*

FALSTAFF *I would your grace would take me with you. Whom means your grace?*

HAL *That villainous, abominable misleader of youth, Falstaff; that old white-bearded Satan.*

FALSTAFF *My lord, the man I know.*

HAL *I know thou dost.*

Gorboduc

If English comedy owed much to Classical models (see page 22), then so too did the tragedies of the mid-16th century. Probably the most well-known tragic play of this period is *Gorboduc* or, as it was called in its second edition, *Ferrex and Porrex*. This was written by Thomas Sackville (1536-1608) and Thomas Norton (1532-84) to be performed at the Inner Temple, one of the Inns of Court, during the Twelfth Night celebrations of Christmas 1561. The play tells the story of the family feuding and subsequent civil war that engulfs the country when the ancient British king, Gorboduc, divides his kingdom between his two sons Ferrex and Porrex while he is still alive. Like *Magnificence*, its subject matter is rule and authority, and although it still owes something to the medieval morality tradition, *Gorboduc* represents a major development towards the Renaissance drama of the 1590s and beyond. *Gorboduc* was the first recorded play to be written in blank verse (unrhymed iambic pentameter), rather than the rhymed verse of earlier dramas. In the following extract, a messenger tells the king that Porrex has killed Ferrex:

Nuntius	O king, the greatest grief that ever prince did hear,
	That ever woeful messenger did tell,
	That ever wretched land hath seen before,
	I bring to you. Porrex, your younger son,
	With sudden force invaded hath the land
	That you to Ferrex did allot to rule;
	And with his own most bloody hand he hath
	His brother slain, and doth possess his realm.
Gorboduc	O heavens, send down the flames of your
	revenge!
	Destroy, I say, with flash of wreakful fire
	The traitor son and then the wretched sire!
	But let us go, that yet perhaps I may
	Die with revenge and 'pease the hateful gods.

Exeunt

Gorboduc was also a landmark in English drama because it was the first 'native' English tragedy, combining the Classical influence of the Roman author Seneca (whose tragedies were the basis for many subsequent English plays) with a contemporary sense of Tudor political thinking. In addition, it started a line of history plays detailing the destiny of England on which Shakespeare was to build in his own plays such as *Richard II* (c.1595), *Henry IV* (c.1597) and *Henry V* (c.1599), and *King Lear* (c.1605). Furthermore, it was the first English play to use dumb show at the beginning of each act to outline the plot that was to follow. A second performance of *Gorboduc* was given at court on 18 January 1562, perhaps

commanded by Queen Elizabeth because the play had broken a
royal edict forbidding plays that touched on politics or religion, and
she wanted to see for herself whether it made any comment on the
succession to her own throne.

Players' companies

The mid-1500s saw religious and secular drama increasingly existing
side by side in the players' repertoire, as the effect of the
Reformation began to bite and as tastes changed. Acting companies
found indoor performances at Easter and Christmas more profitable,
and aspiring or amateur playwrights were more likely to attract
attention from intelligent and well-connected audiences than from
the local populace gathered in the town square. Nevertheless,
summer outdoor performances of mystery plays, mumming plays
(involving St George, an infidel knight, a doctor, Father Christmas
and other stylized characters) and pageants still provided the bread-
and-butter of an actors' living. By the mid-1500s public
performances had moved to inn yards, where the spectators could
stand around the galleries above the yard, and where food and drink
were immediately to hand. Even if there was no permanent
playhouse in existence until 1567, there was a number of
permanent companies of players who toured the major provincial
towns as well as performing in London. Although the touring
companies were all composed of adults, boys' companies such as
the one for whom Udall wrote *Ralph Roister Doister* (see page 22)
were becoming popular, giving regular public performances in their
home towns. The boys for these companies were often drawn from
local grammar schools, or in London from choir schools such as
those of St Paul's Cathedral or the Chapel Royal (see page 38 for
more information about the boys' companies).

The major companies all relied on the protection of a royal or
noble patron, partly as a result of the efforts of the city authorities to
limit or even prevent their activity (see page 36). In 1572 an Act of
Parliament was passed which required any company of actors to
have the endorsement of one nobleman or two members of the
judiciary in order to carry on its trade. Actors without such a patron
would be included with 'all fencers, bearwards [men in charge of
performing bears], common players in interludes & minstrels not
belonging to any Baron of this realm or towards any other person of
greater degree; all jugglers, peddlers, tinkers and petty chapmen…'
and would be 'taken, adjudged and deemed rogues, vagabonds and
sturdy beggars…' and punished accordingly. The Act was tightened
up further in 1598, allowing only noblemen to authorize companies,
and one of James I's first actions on succeeding to the throne in
1603 was to take over the patronage of the three principal
companies in London. The legal requirement for patronage had a

significant impact on the dramatic developments in the capital in the 1580s and '90s, because it increased the competition between companies, which in turn led towards the establishment of permanent theatres, and effectively raised the status of actors – at least the more accomplished ones. (There is more information about the London companies in the next chapter.)

The period between *Gorboduc* (see page 24) and the explosion of the dramatic scene at the beginning of the 1590s was one of transition. Whereas the universities and the Inns of Court had provided the dramatic innovations in the 1560s and '70s, the development of commercial theatres in London and the reliance on royal or noble patronage meant that the physical conditions and the circumstances under which plays were acted were completely new. The first playwrights to make their mark on this scene were sometimes referred to as the 'university wits' – Thomas Lodge (c.1557-1625) and George Peele (1558-96) from Oxford and Robert Greene (c.1558-92), Thomas Nashe (1567-1601) and Christopher Marlowe from Cambridge. These writers had academic backgrounds, but their ability to write plays of quality for the commercial theatre meant that the profile of acting was raised, and so the London theatre continued to gather momentum. Another 'wit' who probably did not attend university, but who is an important figure in the 1580s, was Thomas Kyd (1558-94), author of *The Spanish Tragedy* (c.1589).

A VISIT TO THE THEATRE

There are several panoramic views of the River Thames that provide useful visual information about Renaissance London. The most well-known are by John Norden (1600), J.C. Visscher (1616) (see illustration opposite) and Wenceslaus Hollar (c.1645), in which the public theatres of the South Bank, including the Globe and Hope theatres, can clearly be seen. Although there is also a wealth of archaelogical and written evidence, including lawsuits, letters and diaries, and builders' instructions, there is only one known contemporary pictorial record of the interior of an Elizabethan playhouse, a drawing by the Dutchman Johannes De Witt of the Swan theatre which he made on a visit in 1596 (see illustration on page 43).

The written records of individual productions are similarly rare: there were no newspapers in those days to provide theatre reviews. Thomas Platter, a Swiss traveller staying in London in the autumn of 1599, recorded a visit to a play performance which is of particular significance because it probably describes a production of Shakespeare's Julius Caesar *at the newly-built Globe Theatre:*

'On September 21st after lunch, about two o'clock, I and my party crossed the water, and there in the house with the thatched roof witnessed an excellent performance of the tragedy of the First Emperor Julius Caesar with a cast of some fifteen people; when the play was over, they danced very marvellously and gracefully as is their wont, two dressed as men and two as women...

The playhouses are so constructed that they play on a raised platform, so that everyone has a good view. There are different galleries and places, however, where the seating is better and more comfortable and therefore more expensive. For whoever cares to stand below pays only one English penny, but if he wishes to sit he enters by another door, and pays another penny, while if he wishes to sit in the most comfortable seats which are cushioned, where he not only sees everything well, but can also be seen, then he pays yet another English penny at the door. And during the performance food and drink are carried round the audience, so that for what one cares to pay one may also have refreshment. The actors are most expensively and elaborately costumed; for it is the English usage for eminent lords or knights at their decease to bequeath and leave almost the best of their clothes to their serving men, which it is unseemly for the latter to wear, so that they offer them then for sale for a small sum to the actors.'

Nicholas Visscher,
Panorama of London and the Thames
(engraved c.1615, but published 1660)

Dominating the cityscape is the medieval St Paul's Cathedral, where John Donne became Dean in 1621 (see page 55). In the foreground of the picture, on the south bank of the Thames, are the Beargarden and Globe theatre. The Beargarden was used for bear-baiting, jig dancing and fencing. The owners, Edward Alleyn and Philip Henslowe, replaced it with the Hope playhouse in 1613, designed for both bear-baiting and plays. The original Globe playhouse was built in 1599, but burned down on 29 June 1613, during a performance of Shakespeare's *Henry VIII*.

The Spanish Tragedy was among the most popular plays of its time, and was as influential as Marlowe's *Tamburlaine the Great* (see box) on the theatre of the next decade. Its significance lies in its being the first fully-fledged revenge tragedy (see Glossary of Terms) as well as in the way in which Kyd blended the Classical influence of the Latin tragedian Seneca with his own native style and dramatic structure. Within a very few years Shakespeare would be employing the same technique in his own early plays such as *Titus Andronicus* (c.1590) and *Richard III* (c.1593). Kyd is said to have written a lost version of *Hamlet*, which Shakespeare used as the basis for his own play, first performed in 1600. Even if the earlier play never existed, there is no doubt that Shakespeare was influenced by the revenge theme and Kyd's dramatic methods in *The Spanish Tragedy*. Examples of similarities between the two include the family revenge motive (in this case of an old man for his murdered son, rather than Hamlet's revenge for his murdered father), the presence on stage of the murdered man, and a play-within-a-play which furthers the subsequent action.

Kyd and Marlowe both wrote in a style that was relatively static: characters tend to deliver their speeches in a way that is formal and unrealistic by comparison with the work of Shakespeare and Ben Jonson later in the 1590s. Nevertheless, the rate at which dramatic writing was developing into a subtle and flexible form was extraordinary: playwrights such as Thomas Dekker (c.1570-1632), George Chapman (c.1560-1634), John Marston (1576-1634) and Thomas Heywood (1573-1641) produced plays at a prolific rate besides their other literary activities such as translation, pamphleteering and writing poetry. Rivalry between individual playwrights and between the various

CHRISTOPHER MARLOWE

Christopher Marlowe (1564-93) made an immediate impact with his first play, Tamburlaine the Great, *which was first performed in 1587 and first printed in 1590. The chief reason for the play's considerable success was the vigor of the language and the skill with which Marlowe developed blank verse (first used in drama by Sackville and Norton in* Gorboduc, *see page 24) into a subtle and effective dramatic form. His contemporary, Ben Jonson, described Marlowe's style as a 'mighty line', as illustrated by this speech from* Tamburlaine *in which Tamburlaine himself reflects on the beauty of Zenocrate, whom he marries at the end of the play:*

> 'Ah fair Zenocrate, divine Zenocrate,
> Fair is too foul an epithet for thee,
> That in thy passion for thy country's love,
> And fear to see thy kingly father's harm,
> With hair dishevelled wip'st thy watery cheeks:
> And like to Flora in the morning's pride,
> Shaking her silver tresses in the air,
> Rain'st on earth resolved pearl in showers,
> And sprinklest sapphires on thy shining face,
> Where Beauty, mother to the Muses sits,
> And comments volumes with her ivory pen.'

Marlowe wrote a number of plays in quick succession after Tamburlaine: Tamburlaine Part 2 *(1587),* The Massacre at Paris *(c.1589, based on events in contemporary France, culminating in the St Bartholomew's Day massacre of Parisian Protestants by rival Catholics),* Doctor Faustus *(c.1589),* The Jew of Malta *(c.1590) and* Edward II *(c.1592). He also translated a number of Classical poets, including Ovid's* Amores *(1595), and wrote a long poem called* Hero and Leander *(1598). He achieved rapid fame in a working career of only six years. Marlowe had a strong influence on the early writing of Shakespeare, and some people continue to assert that he was not killed in 1593 (see Biographical Glossary), but lived on to write many of the plays ascribed to Shakespeare.*

theatre companies, and the close attentions of the city authorities to the activities of all the players and the writers associated with them, created a vibrant and stimulating atmosphere in which all genres of drama flourished.

Old and New Comedy

Comedy is a highly individual and varied genre, but there were several specific influences and forms of comedy that predominated in English drama at the turn of the 17th century. Classical drama lay behind the comic writing of the later Elizabethan period, and this was divided into 'Old Comedy' and 'New Comedy'. Old Comedy effectively means the work of Aristophanes, a Greek dramatist of the 5th century BC. Aristophanes' writing is characterised by robust satire of public figures and current affairs in a farcical, often highly unrealistic setting. By the 3rd century BC, however, New Comedy was in vogue. Unlike Old Comedy, which parodied real public figures and events, New Comedy featured fictional, ordinary citizens and took place in familiar urban surroundings. New Comedy was revived in the Renaissance largely through the works of the Roman playwrights Plautus and Terence who had adapted and translated the Greek plays. New Comedy revolved around stock characters such as the cruel father, the cunning servant, the boastful soldier and the beautiful and intelligent daughter. Some Renaissance plays are close adaptations of Roman ones – Shakespeare's *The Comedy of Errors* is one example, as is Udall's *Ralph Roister Doister* – but the influence of Roman comedy can be seen in a lesser way in a large number of other plays, such as Ben Jonson's *Every Man in his Humour* and *The Alchemist*, or Shakespeare's *The Taming of the Shrew*.

Satire

Another significant Classical genre which was revived in the Renaissance was satire. In its distinctive Latin form – the Roman poets Horace, Martial and Juvenal were the models for English Renaissance classical verse – it was a cultured and elegant attack on the moral failings and deficiencies of individual public figures, or of society at large. It implied a civilized and superior standard of behavior on the part of the satirist that allowed him to instruct the rest of society about how to improve. This superiority was often balanced by a more generous form of mockery that tapped a common instinct for comedy. Ben Jonson and John Donne led the revival of satire in English verse from the mid-1590s. In the following satire, 'On Poet-Ape', Jonson draws a typically dry and witty picture of a second-rate playwright (or 'poet') who imitates – apes – other writers' work because he has no ideas of his own:

'Poor Poet-Ape, that would be thought our chief,
Whose works are e'en the frippery of wit,
From brokage is become so bold a thief
As we, the robb'd, leave rage and pity it.
At first he made low shifts, would pick and glean,
Buy the reversion of old plays; now grown
To a little wealth and credit in the scene,
He takes up all, makes each man's wit his own.
And, told of this, he slights it. Tut, such crimes
The sluggish, gaping auditor devours;
He marks not whose 'twas first; and after-times
May judge it to be his, as well as ours.
Fool, as if half eyes will not know a fleece
From locks of wool, or shreds from the whole piece!'

Comedy of humours

From his earliest plays onwards Ben Jonson used comedy as a way of exposing society's follies in a way that was highly topical but which also expressed general truths about greed and vanity. One way in which he did this has become known as the 'comedy of humours'. A comedy of humours takes as its starting point the doctrine of the four humours (see page 10), but Jonson, being a satirist, distorts particular characteristics of his characters so that their 'humours' become all-consuming passions that lead them into social and physical complications. This type of comedy was first employed in George Chapman's *A Humorous Day's Mirth* (1597), and developed by Jonson in plays such as *Every Man in his Humour* (1598), *Every Man out of his Humour* (1599), *The Alchemist* and *The Devil is an Ass*. Other playwrights including Philip Massinger (*A New Way to Pay Old Debts*, 1625) and Thomas Middleton (*A Chaste Maid in Cheapside*, 1613) followed their example.

—— GREEN WORLD COMEDY ——

*Shakespeare's staple comedy in the 1590s was concerned with love and romance in idealized or imaginary places far from the reality of London and England. It is sometimes called 'green world' comedy, because it is set in places such as the wood near Athens (*A Midsummer Night's Dream*) or the Forest of Arden (*As You Like It*), where the normal rules of society do not apply. John Lyly had written plays in this style before Shakespeare took it up; both playwrights drew on Roman comedy and medieval romances for their plots. However, two of Shakespeare's plays (*Love's Labour's Lost* and *A Midsummer Night's Dream*) have no direct source for their plots. In several of Shakespeare's romantic comedies disguise through cross-dressing is an important part of plot and theme, by which Shakespeare dramatizes men's and women's perspectives of love. Another common feature is a sub-plot in which the activities of 'low' characters shadow the manoeuverings of the aristocratic main characters.*

Citizen, or city, comedy

Another aspect of satirical drama initiated by Jonson is sometimes referred to as 'citizen comedy' or 'city comedy'. By the end of the first decade of the 17th century, theatre in London had developed in a manner that could not have been imagined only 20 years

Abraham van Blyernberch,
Ben Jonson (c.1617)

Ben Jonson was one of the strongest personalities of the
Elizabethan theatre, as this portrait of him suggests.
Educated at Westminster School and then apprenticed as a
bricklayer to his stepfather, Jonson was among the most
learned and uncompromising writers of the period. Despite
being imprisoned on several occasions (once for killing a
fellow actor in a brawl, and twice for writing anti-court
satires) he wrote a number of masques for James I's court,
and was awarded an honorary MA by Oxford University. He
famously walked to Edinburgh (and back) to visit William
Drummond of Hawthornden, a Scots poet whom he admired.

before. Theatre-going had become an established cultural activity for all classes, and its growing respectability was signalled by James I's patronage of Shakespeare's own company. The population of London had doubled between 1580 and 1600 as the capital grew in economic and cultural importance and so drew people from other parts of the country. It was entirely natural, therefore, that the city and its life should become the focus of some of the drama being performed to its citizens. In his early plays, Jonson reflected Londoners' preoccupation with money, power and sex in a focused and naturalistic way, and he developed his drama to comment on what he saw as damaging cultural developments. Because his plays, and those of other playwrights such as John Marston and Thomas Middleton (c.1528-1627), were among the first to be so clearly located in the city, and so concerned with what went on in it, they became known as 'city comedies'. The following extract from Middleton's *A Chaste Maid in Cheapside* illustrates the colloquial style and bawdy, bantering idiom. Yellowhammer, a goldsmith, has come across his wife, Maudlin, and daughter, Moll, arguing, and picks up on Maudlin's use of the word 'errors', which he believes to be too smart a word to use in the context:

'**Yellowhammer** Now, what's the din betwixt mother and
                        daughter, ha?
Maudlin   Faith, small, telling your daughter Mary of her
                        errors.
Yellowhammer 'Errors', nay the city cannot hold you, wife, but
                        you must needs fetch your words from
                        Westminster; I ha' done, i'faith. Has no
                        attorney's clerk been here a-late and changed
                        his half-crown-piece his mother sent him, or
                        rather cozened [cheated] you with a gilded
                        twopence, to bring the word in fashion for her
                        faults or cracks in duty and obedience, term
                        'em e'en so, sweet wife? As there is no
                        woman made without a flaw, your purest lawns
                        [fine linens] have frays, and cambrics bracks
                        [faults].
Maudlin   But 'tis a husband solders up all cracks.
Moll   What, is he come, sir?
Yellowhammer Sir Walter's come.
                        He was met at Holborn Bridge, and in his
                        company
                        A proper fair young gentlewoman, which I
                        guess
                        By her red hair, and other rank descriptions,

> To be his landed niece brought out of Wales,
> Which Tim our son (the Cambridge boy) must
> marry.'

Another city comedy that functions as a celebration is *The Shoemaker's Holiday* by Thomas Dekker, first performed in 1599 at the Rose playhouse. Dekker dramatizes in a cheerful and romantic way the story of Simon Eyre, a historical character from the mid-15th century, a shoemaker who becomes Lord Mayor of London. The play's nostalgic view of the past is similar to that of Shakespeare's *Henry V,* first performed in the same year, and it is probably no coincidence that the shoemakers' main holiday, which is given prominence in the play, was St Hugh's Day, 17 November – the date of Elizabeth's accession to the throne. Dekker could indulge in gentle flattery (the play was performed at court in the queen's presence on New Year's Day 1600) just as well as he could satirize the wealthy citizens of London in his pamphlets (see page 66).

Tragedy

Seneca provided the Classical antecedents for English tragedy, but Marlowe, Shakespeare, Middleton and John Webster (c.1580-c.1634) wrote in a manner that was entirely their own. Building on Classical convention, their tragic heroes are men of high position and authority who are undone by a combination of character and circumstance. In their tragedies they juxtaposed the Classical ideas of fickle gods and the necessity of revenge with a Christian understanding of salvation and God as the ultimate dispenser of justice. This Christian understanding is summed up in a passage from Chapter 7 of St Matthew's Gospel in the Bible (which provided Shakespeare with the title of his play *Measure for Measure,* c.1604):

> 'Judge not, that ye be not judged. For with what
> judgment ye judge, ye shall be judged: and with what
> measure ye mete, it shall be measured to you again.'

Where non-Shakespearean comedy tended to be rooted in contemporary London, tragedy was often set in other times and places: Spain or, more commonly, Italy were favorite locations because of the associations with the bloody, corrupt and immoral practices of the Continent, and in particular of the Borgias, Medici and the incarnation of evil, Machiavelli himself (see page 60). Ancient Rome was another common setting (*Julius Caesar* [1599], *Antony and Cleopatra* [c.1607] and *Coriolanus* [c.1608] by Shakespeare, *Sejanus* [1603] and *Catiline* [1611] by Jonson, and *Caesar and Pompey* by George Chapman, for example). In the course of James I's reign, tragic writing became darker and more preoccupied with the psychology of corruption: the work of John Ford (*'Tis Pity She's a Whore,* printed 1633) and Thomas Middleton (*Women Beware Women,* 1621 and *The Changeling,* 1622) touched on areas of sexuality and depravity that would have been unthinkable in the 1580s and '90s.

Masque

During the reigns of James I and Charles I the masque reached its high point. Masque was a form that had originated in Europe during the early Renaissance, characterized by elaborate costumes, formal dancing and music, and elaborate stage scenery and machinery. It arrived in England during the Tudor period, and became popular during the reign of Elizabeth. During the 1570s and '90s Elizabeth toured the country, staying at the stately homes of the local aristocracy, and it became customary for her hosts to put on entertainments to express their joy and honour at her arrival. The nobility sometimes went to extraordinary lengths to attract the queen's approval. Sir John Young specially built a mansion large enough to accommodate Elizabeth when she visited the city of Bristol in 1574; at Kenilworth in 1575 the castle clock was stopped for the duration of her stay; while at Bedington in 1599 Sir Francis Carew delayed the flowering of the cherry trees so that they would appear to come into bloom as a result of Elizabeth's arrival. During the queen's stay, lavish performances would be mounted, usually based on mythological or allegorical plots which linked Elizabeth to idealized embodiments of her majesty such as Gloriana, the Fairy Queen or Cynthia, the goddess of the Moon. At Kenilworth in 1591, for example, an artifical lake was created, on which a miniature sea-battle was fought, and a mythological water pageant, involving mermaids, dolphins and tritons, was performed.

The Renaissance mind loved symbolism or iconography, and masques invariably presented allegorical characters or situations to stand for the patron or monarch for whom the entertainment was prepared. By the time of the early Stuart monarchs (James I and Charles I), masque performances had moved indoors, to royal halls such as the Banqueting House at Whitehall (see illustration opposite), where the elaborate stage designs and machinery could be prepared and set up at leisure. Inigo Jones (1573-1652) was the greatest designer of masques, and his collaboration with Ben Jonson over many years resulted in a number of spectacular but conspicuously extravagant masques. One particular feature of Jones's designs was the introduction of the proscenium arch, which was to become an important element in English theatre for several centuries to come.

The Banqueting House, Whitehall, Inigo Jones, completed 1622

Designed by Inigo Jones for James I, the Banqueting House at Whitehall Palace is a very early example of neo-Classical architecture in England. It was the scene of frequent entertainments and masques, many written by Ben Jonson to designs by Inigo Jones himself. The collaboration between the two men had broken down by 1634, neither one able to acknowledge the superior role of the other in the creation of their masques.

3. THE SHAKESPEAREAN THEATRE

The fixed stage

In the early 1570s in London there was a number of acting companies known by their patron's name, such as the Earl of Pembroke's Men, the Earl of Sussex's Men and The Earl of Leicester's Men. None of these companies had a permanent base, but were reliant on inn-yards and the halls of private houses and the Inns of Court for their performances. The major disadvantage of these temporary venues was financial: the players did not have captive audiences that they could charge for their performances, and so were unlikely ever to attract the money necessary to improve the quality of their art form. However, the combination of significant investment in a number of new permanent playhouses, the emergence of a group of young men such as Kyd, Marlowe and the other 'university wits' interested in writing for the commercial theatre (see page 26), and the effect of the security and stability of Elizabeth's reign all led to the transformation of the Elizabethan theatre by the end of the century.

The Corporation of London was deeply suspicious of the players. This was partly because it was inclined to support Puritan values and therefore disapproved of public performance in general, but also because it perceived the playhouses as encouraging rowdy, anti-social behavior – including absenteeism from work – and as a seed-bed of crime, corruption and the plague. The Corporation was able to restrict the activities of the acting companies within its own jurisdiction, but it could do little to prevent a handful of theatre proprietors from seizing the opportunity to build up business outside the city limits. For these reasons, the playhouses that grew up from 1576 onwards were all built outside the legal jurisdiction of the City, primarily at Bankside, on the south bank of the Thames. Although the Lord Mayor and the Corporation tried repeatedly to restrain the influence of the playhouses by appealing to the Privy Council (Elizabeth's government), the players were generally looked on favorably by the queen and her court. Indeed, in 1583 Elizabeth, through the agency of Sir Francis Walsingham, established the Queen's Men, employing several of the best actors from other companies to start the new company. The motivation behind this venture, besides showing the queen's obvious approval of contemporary theatre, was to allay the rivalry between existing companies and their patrons in the increasingly heated atmosphere of the court. Nevertheless, the Privy Council did step in on occasions to curb the excesses and enthusiasms of those playwrights and actors who overstepped the mark, and reacted strongly to any dramatic performance that hinted of sedition.

The Admiral's Men

The make-up and patronage of actors' companies constantly changed as circumstances altered, but by 1594 two adult companies had established their pre-eminence in London: the Admiral's Men and the Chamberlain's Men (there were also two well-established boys' companies – see page 38). The Admiral's Men started off as Lord Howard's Men, named after their patron Lord Howard of Effingham, who became Lord High Admiral in 1585 (and who commanded the English fleet against the Spanish Armada in 1588). They were financed by Philip Henslowe (d.1616), the most influential theatre manager of the period, and their reputation was due in no small measure to the presence in the company of Edward Alleyn (1566-1626), who was considered the finest actor of the day. A number of the plays of Christopher Marlowe, including *Doctor Faustus* and *Tamburlaine* were first performed by the Admiral's Men, and under the dual leadership of Alleyn and Henslowe (Alleyn shrewdly married Henslowe's step-daughter in 1592 to seal their relationship) the company enjoyed considerable success from the 1590s until the early years of the 17th century, when Alleyn's retirement and the rise of the Chamberlain's Men altered its fortunes.

The Chamberlain's Men

The Chamberlain's Men emerged out of a re-shuffling of theatrical talent between 1592 and 1594. Before that period the dominant adult companies in London were the Queen's Men, Lord Strange's Men (under the patronage of Ferdinando Stanley, 5th Earl of Derby, but known as Lord Strange) and the Admiral's Men. In 1590, the Admiral's and Lord Strange's Men merged, although they probably continued to tour the provinces separately under their own names. The combined company used James Burbage's playhouse, the Theatre (see page 39), to present plays, but as a result of disagreements between Burbage and Henslowe, a number of the players moved in 1592 to a new venue, the Rose playhouse, which was owned and managed by Henslowe. The London theatres were closed from 1592 to 1594 because of the plague, and by the summer of 1594, some unknown factor had caused the break-up of the Queen's Men, and the formation under the patronage of Henry Carey, Lord Hunsdon, of the Chamberlain's Men.

The Chamberlain's Men included both James Burbage and his son Richard in its ranks, as well as John Heminges and Henry Condell (the editors of the First Folio of Shakespeare's works) and the clowns William Kemp (see illustration page 41) and Robert Armin. Shakespeare may have been a member of the Earl of Pembroke's Men or Lord Strange's Men at the start of his career, and he may have confined himself to writing poetry during the playhouses and hired a builder secretly to remove the timbers of the Theatre (incurring the wrath of the landlord, who sued for trespass) and transport them over London Bridge to Bankside. The new theatre was named the Globe. The Chamberlain's Men used it as their base for many years and most of Shakespeare's subsequent plays were written specifically for the venue.

Since much of their wealth was still tied up in the Blackfriars hall playhouse, the cost of the Globe project was such that the Burbages took the unprecedented step of sharing it among members of the acting company. The brothers bore half the expense, and five actors in the Chamberlain's Men – Shakespeare, Augustine Phillips, Thomas Pope, John Heminges and William Kemp – took a ten per cent stake each. In due course, Kemp withdrew his share, which was bought up by the other four. Being tied to the running and management of the theatre was a risk for the new 'sharers', but the return from the box-office receipts as well as the general fortunes of the company proved to be a very worthwhile investment for Shakespeare – much more so than the payments that he received for the plays themselves (see page 48).

Philip Henslowe: the Rose and the Fortune

The Rose was the first of the theatres to be completed at Bankside, on the south bank of the Thames in the borough of Southwark. This was the work of Philip Henslowe, who had married a wealthy widow and used her money to buy property in Southwark and its environs. Southwark had technically been incorporated into the City of London in 1550, but the area had for centuries been known for its brothels and other places of entertainment, and for its criminals. Henslowe's new theatre was built in the yard of the Rose brothel, which Henslowe probably kept going to increase the revenue from the property (he and Edward Alleyn also had interests in other brothels in the neighborhood). The land on which it stood was, as stated, theoretically under the jurisdiction of the City of London, but was within the 'liberty' of the Clink prison and therefore free from the City's regulation.

Henslowe built the Rose in 1587, but it is not known whether it was used as a playhouse, or for bearbaiting or other popular entertainment. In 1592, in order to accommodate the Admiral's Men as a resident company, Henslowe renovated and enlarged it to increase the size of the auditorium and to provide more space on the stage, turning the regular polygonal ground plan into a stretched and asymmetrical oval. The building of the Swan playhouse (see page 42) nearby in 1595-6 did not affect the success of the Rose, but the arrival of the Chamberlain's Men at the Globe in 1599 must have had an adverse effect on Henslowe's business, since in 1600 he built a

Title page of Kemp's *Nine Daies Wonder* (1600)

William Kemp was a successful theatrical clown in the 1590s, working with Shakespeare's own company, the Chamberlain's Men. He was an expert at singing and dancing jigs, and is known to have played the part of Dogbery in *Much Ado About Nothing* (c.1595) and Peter in *Romeo and Juliet* (c.1598). After he left the Chamberlain's Men in 1599 he danced a morris dance from London to Norwich for a bet. He published a pamphlet commemorating his morris dance, and is shown here on the title page dancing to the accompaniment of pipe and drum.

Kemps nine daies vvonder.

Performed in a daunce from
London to Norwich.

Containing the pleaſure, paines and kinde entertainment
of *William Kemp* betweene *London* and that Citty
in his late Morrice.

Wherein is ſomewhat ſet downe worth note; to reprooue
the ſlaunders ſpred of him: many things merry,
nothing hurtfull.

Written by himſelfe to ſatisfie his friends.

LONDON
Printed by *E.A.* for *Nicholas Ling,* and are to be
ſolde at his ſhop at the weſt doore of Saint
Paules Church. 1600.

(the backstage area) in the yard, but the building was enlarged and re-shaped in 1599 in order to maximize its capacity. The theatre never really attracted a great following – even though it was the only playhouse on record to possess an indoor privy – and it had run its course by 1604. In that same year a new inn conversion, the Red Bull, opened in Clerkenwell, a north-eastern suburb of the city, with much greater success. There the revived Queen's Men played, performing new plays by Thomas Heywood and John Webster until they moved to the Cockpit in 1616 (see page 45).

The later playhouses: Blackfriars and the Hope

After the failure to use the Blackfriars hall playhouse in 1597 as the base for the Chamberlain's Men (see page 39), Richard and Cuthbert Burbage concentrated their efforts on the Globe. However, they never surrendered their interest in the land at Blackfriars. From 1600, they leased it to Henry Evans, who had revived the Children of the Chapel Royal under the new name of the Chapel Children (see page 38). Presumably the residents were less worried by the effect on the neighborhood of a private children's company than a public adult one, and Evans's venture was successful for several years until the controversy of Chapman's *Byron* plays (see page 38) caused the boys' company to relocate. Although Evans still had several years of the lease to run on Blackfriars, he had little choice but to surrender the playhouse back to the Burbage brothers. They immediately took it over as a second venue for the Chamberlain's Men, who in 1603 had been renamed the King's Men when King James became their patron.

———— LEADING ACTORS ————

Edward Alleyn was born in 1566, the son of a London innkeeper. He started acting early, serving with Worcester's Men until he joined the Admiral's Men when his reputation was already well established. He was particularly associated with the tragic roles of Christopher Marlowe's plays – Tamburlaine, Doctor Faustus and The Jew of Malta – and the character of Orlando in Orlando Furioso (c. 1591) by Robert Greene. Alleyn described himself as 'the fustian king', referring to his pompous, bombastic style of delivery, but he was a shrewd businessman as well as a great actor. With his fortune he bought the manor of Dulwich in south London, and in 1613 began the foundation of a school and a hospital which still survive as Dulwich College, James Allen's Girls' School and Alleyn's School.

Richard Burbage is well-known for his involvement with the Chamberlain's Men in building the Globe theatre and as their manager and majority shareholder, but in the 1590s he was better known as the chief rival of Alleyn for the claim to be the greatest actor of the day. As the lead actor of the Chamberlain's/King's Men he played the parts of many Shakespearean tragic heroes including Richard III, Hamlet, King Lear and Othello, as well as Hieronimo in Kyd's The Spanish Tragedy and Ferdinand in Webster's The Duchess of Malfi, which was first performed at the Blackfriars hall playhouse in 1613.

Two of the best-known boy actors of the time were Nathaniel Field and Salomon Pavy. Field worked for the Children of the Chapel Royal from around 1600 onwards, and then joined the King's Men in 1616 at the age of 29, possibly to replace Shakespeare. For three years he and Burbage were linked as equals, until their deaths in 1619. Salomon Pavy was another actor in the Chapel Children, known for his playing of old men. Ben Jonson, who wrote Cynthia's Revels (1600) for the company, composed an epitaph on his death in 1602 at the age of 13:

'... 'Twas a child that so did thrive
In grace and feature,
As Heaven and Nature seemed to strive
Which owned the creature.
Years he numbered scarce thirteen
When Fates turned cruel,
Yet three filled zodiacs had he been
The stage's jewel.'

Attitudes had changed since 1597 (see page 39), and in 1608 the King's Men were allowed to use the Blackfriars theatre without objection from the locals or the authorities, even though the land was by that time under the direct jurisdiction of the Corporation. Having a second, indoor, theatre was a great advantage to the company. It was much more accessible to a wealthier audience, who were charged more for entry than at the Globe (a minimum of 6*d* [pence] as opposed to 1*d*). It was protected from the elements, so that that the King's Men could use the Globe during the summer months and then re-locate to Blackfriars for a winter 'season'. It also allowed for a more intimate, more subtle drama than was possible in the large open spaces of the amphitheatre at the Globe. It is likely that Shakespeare's later plays *Pericles* (1608), *Cymbeline* (1609)*, The Winter's Tale* (1610) and *The Tempest* (1611) were all written for first performance at Blackfriars. These were romances – blending tragic and comic elements in a way Shakespeare had not used before – and the change in style and genre from the major tragedies which he had written during the first decade of the new century for performances at the Globe can be partly explained by the acquisition of the new theatre.

The Blackfriars theatre was much smaller than the Globe, for actors and audience alike. It contained an auditorium with a pit. Seats or benches were provided for the audience, and there were also boxes arranged around the walls, supporting galleries above. The acting area was probably set against one of the shorter walls, with a tiring house and a 'room over the stage' for machinery and a balcony for musicians. Since the stage was lit by candles, it might have been possible to create effects with lighting, and the evidence of Shakespeare's late plays suggests that relatively sophisticated effects with staging and machinery were also possible. In short, the overall experience at the Blackfriars must have been nearer to what we consider a conventional theatre than anywhere else at the time. The precedent set by the King's Men at the Blackfriars hall playhouse was imitated in other 'hall' theatres elsewhere in the city: at the Whitefriars, the Cockpit in Drury Lane (adapted in 1616 from a cock-fighting pit, possibly to designs by Inigo Jones, in order to get round restrictions on building new theatres) and Salisbury Court, built in 1629.

The Burbage brothers and the other sharers in the King's Men had made a success of their ventures by 1610. The Admiral's Men (renamed Prince Henry's Men in 1603) continued to perform at the Fortune, but in 1614, Henslowe and Alleyn (who had retired from acting in the first decade of the new century and confined himself to theatre management) moved back to Bankside, possibly to capitalize on the burning of the Globe in the previous year. Near the site of the Rose theatre (demolished in 1606) the two men replaced their existing South Bank enterprise, the Beargarden (see illustration on page 27), with the Hope playhouse, designed to act as a dual-purpose venue for plays and for bull- and bear-baiting. However, the scheme was not a great success, and by the time of Alleyn's death in 1626, the players had lost out and the building was given over exclusively to animal-baiting.

Playwrights and publishing

Shakespeare retired from the London theatre at some point between 1611 and 1613 and retired to Stratford-on-Avon as a wealthy man. He had made his money as a result of being a sharer in the Chamberlain's Men, not through his writing, which is suggested by the fact that he himself had no recorded interest in the publication of his plays during his lifetime. Ben Jonson, by comparison, was a freelance writer and actor without the financial security that Shakespeare enjoyed as a sharer, and in 1616 he took the unprecedented step of publishing his complete *Works* in a lavish folio edition. Jonson clearly wanted to retain control of his plays by publishing them on his terms – he was closely involved in the printing process and spent much time reading and correcting the proofs prior to their final publication – and to proclaim the worth of his art as a playwright and poet to the book-buying public. Jonson was ridiculed by some of his contemporaries for his presumption in undertaking the venture, and for giving his plays the dignified status of 'Works' (normally reserved for more serious forms of writing), but Shakespeare's own plays were accorded the same treatment seven years later (see box page 48).

Some playwrights, such as Marlowe, Shakespeare and Thomas Heywood (who wrote for Queen Anne's Men at the Red Bull), were contracted by a company to act as its resident playwright or 'poet'. Others, like Jonson and most of his contemporaries, worked as hack writers, selling plays to whichever company was willing to stage them and being paid a fee for the script. Most, if not all, playwrights also wrote in other forms – masques, poetry, pamphlets or translations of foreign texts, for example – and were often actors as well.

A significant proportion of plays were collaborations between two or more playwrights. Francis Beaumont (1584-1616) and John Fletcher (1579-1625) were probably the most successful team, writing a number of tragicomedies and romances for the Blackfriars hall playhouse. The three writers patronised by the Chapel Children – Jonson, Chapman and Marston – all had a hand in *Eastward Ho!* (1605), a satire that included references to King James's Scottish favorites at court; Jonson and Chapman were both imprisoned, despite their protests that the offensive parts had been written by Marston. Thomas Middleton collaborated with Webster, Dekker and others, and notably joined forces with William Rowley (c.1585-1626), who is believed to have written the comic sub-plot of *The Changeling*. Shakespeare probably worked with John Fletcher to an unknown extent in the writing of *Henry VIII* (1613) and *The Two Noble Kinsmen* (1613-4).

The prevalence of such collaboration also lends weight to the view that writers were not unduly concerned about the authorship of their plays in their own right: the performance (and the commercial ability to control that performance) was more important than the text itself, which was treated as a relatively ephemeral medium in Elizabethan times. This state of affairs came about partly because the copy of the play was owned by the acting company, but also because the close relationship between the poet and the company meant that the script might well be amended and adapted in the course of rehearsal, and there was not, therefore, a single definitive version of the play. The traditionally lowly status accorded to the theatre and those associated with it also contributed to this indifference to the fate of manuscripts and the written integrity of a playwright's work.

From plot to print

For all these reasons the great majority of Elizabethan and Jacobean plays have survived only in the form of printed texts rather than the original manuscripts, though the means by which a play travelled from the playwright's original conception to the stage and then into print was the same in most instances.

The author probably first drew up a preliminary outline of the sequence of scenes, or 'plot', and used this to write a first draft of the play, known as the 'foul papers'. Little value was attached to this stage of the writing process, and very few foul papers survive. The details of exits and entrances, stage directions and even some characters were often only sketched in, and the text would not have been in any sense a fair copy of the play. The foul papers were then usually transcribed neatly for use as a prompt-book, either by the author or by a scribe. Any inaccuracies in transcription were relatively unimportant, since the author was probably available in rehearsal to clear up uncertainties about the text.

The term 'prompt-book', more often called simply 'the book', referred to the copy used by the company in the preparation of the play's production. It was the manuscript from which individual actors' parts were copied for them to learn their lines. It was the copy of the play from which the rehearsal schedule and lists of exits and entrances, props and special effects were prepared. It was also held by the 'book-keeper' in rehearsals and performances to prompt actors who forgot their lines.

Before the play could be performed it had to be licensed by the

Master of the Revels, an official working for the Lord Chamberlain on behalf of the Privy Council. His authorization was given to the prompt-book once any censorship of over-sensitive political or topical references had been carried out. For this reason the prompt-book was valuable, as it gave its owner the right to perform the play. When Shakespeare joined the Chamberlain's Men in 1594 he brought with him the prompt-books of several plays written earlier in his career, which suggests that he had broken with the general rule that the playwright sold his play to the company for which it was written, and had kept the books as a valuable commodity.

Once it had been performed, a play was sometimes copied for the private enjoyment of an individual friend or patron of the poet, but this was expensive and was not widespread practice. Thomas Middleton's *A Game at Chess* (1624) was copied in manuscript several times because the play had been banned after nine performances and its notoriety made it a valuable commodity. On such occasions copying was with the author's consent, and the copy made from either the foul papers or the prompt-book. However, illegal manuscript reconstructions written down at performances were also fairly common, as were versions made from memory by unscrupulous actors trying to make some extra cash by selling them to other companies.

The value of a play lay in its performance and so companies were careful to look after their copies of plays. Nevertheless, many manuscripts did make it into print. This might be for various reasons: either because an impoverished playwright sold a second copy of his play to a printer; or because a play's popularity made it difficult to keep the text within the confines of the playhouse; or because the company wanted to correct the text of a pirated version (as was the case with *Hamlet*, for example); or because the

——— THE FIRST FOLIO ———

None of Shakespeare's own literary manuscripts has survived, and so his work has been passed down only in print. Almost half of the plays were printed for the first time after his death, and there is no evidence that he oversaw or had any involvement in the printing of the others. Since he was actively involved in every aspect of the work of the Chamberlain's and King's Men, he would have written each play in the awareness that he would be present at rehearsals to interpret and alter it if necessary, and it was never intended to be a single definitive document.

Shakespeare died in 1616, and two of his friends and fellow-actors, John Heminges and Henry Condell, set about collecting all his plays into a single memorial edition. This was to be a particularly special publication, and they therefore chose to present it in folio format (see Glossary of Terms), as Ben Jonson had done. However, where Jonson had prepared the texts for publication himself, Heminges and Condell were reliant upon any suviving manuscripts and printed editions of Shakespeare's work without, obviously, access to the opinions of the man himself. The path to publication in the First Folio (which was entered in the Stationers' Register in 1623) was therefore different for each separate play, but the editors probably tended to use transcripts or existing editions in preference to the foul papers, using the prompt-books where further information was necessary. In the case of some plays the Folio is the first printed edition of the text; in others, there were several quarto versions (see Glossary of Terms), and the integrity of these plays is therefore likely to be more questionable, since the texts had already undergone alteration on their way to each printing. There was possibly no overall editorial policy, the choice of sources depending upon how readily available a particular version of a play was, and there are plenty of variations of editorial practice within the First Folio.

Title page of 'Mr William Shakespeare's Comedies, Histories and Tragedies' (the First Folio), engraving by Martin Droeshout (1623)

The First Folio was published seven years after Shakespeare's death as a memorial to him by his fellow actors and shareholders in the King's Men, John Heminges and Henry Condell. The collection contained 36 plays, including 17 which had not been printed before. The illustration, by Martin Droeshout, who was 15 when Shakespeare died, is probably not a good representation, but has endured as the definitive image of the playwright.

William Shakespeare, Act I Scene I of *Hamlet* in the First Folio (1623)

There were two printed versions of *Hamlet* (1600) before it appeared in the First Folio. The earliest one, known as the 'Bad Quarto', was an unauthorized production published in 1603, intended to capitalize on the success of the play when it was first performed. It may well have been constructed from the memory of the actor playing the part of Marcellus, who appears in the opening scene of the play, shown here. The King's Men quickly brought out an 'authorized' quarto edition in 1604 to set the record straight.

play had run its course and the company could make more money by selling it than by keeping it on their books. Generally, though, published editions of plays at this time were not sanctioned by theatrical companies.

Individual plays were sold in quarto format, which was a relatively cheap form of book, usually selling for 6*d*. The copyright to a work was held not by the author, but by the publisher, or stationer, who would register his interest in the centrally maintained Stationers' Register and obtain a licence to print the book from the Archbishop of Canterbury and the Bishop of London, or their deputies. If it was an authorized edition the publisher might use any of the available manuscripts as the basis for the text. Obviously the foul papers or the prompt-book (with any later emendations) would result in a more accurate edition than, say, a reconstruction based on an actor's recollection of individual parts, or one simply pirated from an existing printed edition of the play.

4 . P R O S E

The bedrock of the development of the English language in the Renaissance was prose, the daily means of communication of ideas and feelings. Although the drama and poetry of the period are more memorable and more frequently studied, prose texts, and particularly the Bible, were no less influential on the people and the times.

Some mention has already been made (see box page 16) of the first publications in English at Caxton's press in Westminster, from 1476 onwards. After Caxton's death in 1491, a system of trade restrictions and strict licensing was put in place by the government to protect the printing industry against foreign competition and unskilled operators. One consequence of the close attention of the Crown was that the content of the books produced by the printers was strictly controlled, and power was vested in the archbishops of Canterbury and London to license every publication. Inevitably, the printing industry was often linked to political or religious controversy as it attempted to reflect popular concerns and issues which Crown and Church preferred to keep suppressed.

Translations of the Bible

In particular, the status of the Bible aroused considerable debate. Many in authority believed that the Bible should not be translated into the vernacular (the native language of a particular country), since the classical languages of Greek and Latin were the only ones solemn enough to convey the meaning of the Bible. There had been, nevertheless, translations in manuscript form of the Bible into English long before the 16th century. In the 8th century, the Anglo-Saxon scholar and poet Bede (c.673-735) translated the gospels (completed 735), while in 1381-2 John Wyclif (c.1320-84) and his followers (known as the Lollards) translated the complete Bible in support of Wyclif's radical theological view that the Church had grown too powerful, and could not be said to represent God's purpose on Earth. By translating the Vulgate Bible (a Latin version of the original Hebrew and Greek, completed by Saint Jerome in 405) into English, Wyclif aimed to give literate individuals the power to read and understand the Scriptures without the involvement of the Church. The translation provoked a storm of reaction, and Wyclif's works were banned. Reprisals against the Lollards, who maintained Wyclif's anti-Church views, continued after his death in 1384, and a number were burned at the stake for heresy.

In the 1520s, William Tyndale (c.1494-1536), an academic and theologian, became convinced, as Wyclif had before him, that lay people (those not ordained as priests or bishops in the Church) were entitled to read the Bible in their own language, since the

Scripture alone – and not the interpretation of it by the Church for its own purposes – should be the guide for ordinary people. Prevented by the Church from publishing in England, he moved to the Continent and succeeded in having his translation of the New Testament printed in Cologne in 1525. Unlike earlier translators, who had used the Vulgate Bible, Tyndale referred back to the original Greek and Hebrew sources (as did Martin Luther in his German translations of 1522-34). Tyndale was working on a translation of the Old Testament when he was captured and executed for heresy in 1536.

Tyndale's New Testament was the first English Bible translation to be printed; one of the collaborators in that enterprise, Miles Coverdale (c.1488-1569), is credited with the publication of the first complete printed Bible in English, published in Zurich in 1535 (see illustration page 57). A version that combined the work of both men, known as the Great Bible, was issued for use in English churches in 1539 after Henry VIII had broken from Rome (in 1534, see page 7). It was a result of Henry's desire to establish the separate identity of the English Church. Ten years later, in 1549, Edward VI commissioned Thomas Cranmer, Archbishop of Canterbury, to make the first English version of the liturgy, entitled *The Book of Common Prayer*. During the reign of Mary I another English translation, more widely-used than the Great Bible and known as the Geneva Bible, was prepared by Protestants exiled from England. After Mary's strict and repressive reign, official attitudes to the English Bible and liturgy were relaxed again under Elizabeth I and James I. But the translators of the Geneva Bible had been influenced by Calvinist theories (see page 6), and the Elizabethan bishops felt that aspects of the Geneva Bible, popular though it was, gave its readers too much of a hard-line Protestant interpretation of the Scriptures. They therefore

— TWO VERSIONS OF THE BIBLE —

The differences between the direct, everyday language of Tyndale's version of the New Testament and the more carefully phrased, formal Authorised Version, known as the King James Bible, can be seen in the comparison of a passage from St Matthew, Chapter 6:

Tyndale's New Testament (1525)

And when ye praye, bable not moche, as the hethen do: for they thincke thay they shall be herde, for their moche bablynges sake. Be ye not lyke them therefore. For your father knoweth wherof ye have neade, before ye axe of him. After thys maner therefore praye ye.

O oure father which arte in heven, halowed be thy name. Let thy knygdome come. Thy wyll be fulfilled, as well in erth, as it ys in heven. Geve us thisdaye oure dayly breede. And forgeve us oure treaspases, even as we forgeve oure trespacers. And leade us not into temptacion: but delyver us from evell. For thyne is the kygedome and the power and the glorye for ever. Amen.

The Authorised Version (1611)

But when ye pray, use not vain repetitions, as the heathen do: for they think that they shall be heard for their much speaking. Be not ye therefore like unto them: for your Father knoweth what things ye have need of, before ye ask him. After this manner therefore pray ye:

Our Father which art in heaven, Hallowed be thy name. Thy kingdom come. Thy will be done in earth, as it is in heaven. Give us this day our daily bread. And forgive us our debts, as we forgive our debtors. And lead us not into temptation, but deliver us from evil: For thine is the kingdom, and the power, and the glory, for ever. Amen.

issued yet another English translation which presented a more conservative slant, known as the Bishops' Bible (1568).

In 1604, James I commissioned 47 scholars to produce an 'official' translation of the Bible to end the competing claims of the various versions in use throughout the country. The culmination of their work was the Authorized Version, completed in 1611, which took as its starting point the version by Tyndale as well as going back to the original languages. The Authorized Version had a style and quality which led to centuries of use before it was revised in the 1880s.

Other religious writing

Foxe's *Book of Martyrs*

Many Elizabethan households possessed a copy of a book which was second only to the Bible as a religious text. This was *Acts and monuments of these Latter and Perilous Days*, which was invariably referred to by its popular name, *The Book of Martyrs*. It was compiled by John Foxe (1516-87) and first published in Latin in 1559. A scholar and staunch Protestant, Foxe had begun the book at the start of the 1550s, but was forced abroad by the accession of Mary Tudor in 1553. The book was ostensibly a record of Christian martyrs from earliest times, but by Christian martyrs, Foxe meant those who had refused to comply with the 'false' faith of the Catholic Church. The first English edition, published in 1563, was immediately a huge success. In order to reinforce the impact of the text, Foxe collaborated with the printer John Day to produce illustrations to accompany the vivid descriptions of burnings and hangings of Protestants.

Like Machiavelli's *The Prince* (see page 60), Foxe's *Book of Martyrs* encouraged a very one-sided English Protestant hatred of Catholics and the corruption and evil of the Continent. In the following description of the burning of Thomas Cranmer for his part in the plot to put Lady Jane Grey on the throne (see page 7), the dignity of Cranmer's behavior is strongly contrasted with the behavior of his Catholic persecutors:

'And then Cranmer, being pulled down from the seat, was led to the fire, accompanied with those friars, vexing, troubling, and threatening him most cruelly. What madness (say they) hath brought thee again into this error, by which thou wilt draw innumerable souls with thee into hell? To whom he answered nothing, but directed all his talk to the people, saving that to one troubling him in the way, he spake and exhorted him to get him home to his study and apply his book diligently, saying that if he did not diligently call upon God, by reading more he should get knowledge. But the other Spanish barker, raging and foaming, was almost out of his wits, always having this in his mouth, *Non fecisti?* Didst thou it not?

But when he came to the place where the holy bishops and martyrs of god, Hugh Latimer and Ridley, were burnt before him for confession of the truth, kneeling down, he prayed to God, and, not long tarrying in his prayers, putting off his garments to his shirt, he prepared himself to death.'

Richard Hooker

Foxe's book was deliberately written in a lurid style which contrasts with that of the leading theologians and intellectuals of the day. Perhaps the most outstanding piece of theological writing of the English Renaissance was the *Laws of Ecclesiastical Polity* (1594-7) written by Richard Hooker (c.1554-1600), master of the Temple Church in the Inns of Court. Hooker was a moderate churchman during a time when there was much debate about the direction in which the English Church should go. The defeat of the Armada in 1588 had ended the Catholic threat to Britain, but the Church of England was also under pressure from Puritans within its own ranks. They believed that the English Church was too similar in its structure and faith to the Roman Church, and that it should be reformed further, in line with radical continental thinking. The Catholic Church put reliance both on the authority of Scripture and on traditions evolved over the centuries; extreme Protestant doctrine claimed that Scripture alone was the basis for faith. Hooker argued for a middle, humanist, way: where there was a conflict between convention and Scripture, he argued that mankind should obey reason and observe the laws of nature to resolve the conflict. He also argued in favor of the settlement arrived at under Elizabeth, that the Church and the state were inseparable, and that loyalty to the monarch was a natural consequence of loyalty to God. The following extract from the first book of the *Laws of Ecclesiastical Polity* illustrates the balanced rhetorical style characteristic of Hooker:

'Where understanding therefore needeth, in those things Reason is the director of man's Will by discovering in action what is good. For the Laws of well-doing are the dictates of right Reason. Children, which are not as yet come unto those years whereat they may have; again, innocents, which are excluded by natural defect from ever having; thirdly, madmen, which for the present cannot possibly have the use of right Reason to guide themselves, have for their guide the Reason that guideth other men, which are tutors

over them to seek and to procure their good for them.
In the rest is the light of Reason, whereby good
maybe known from evil, and which discovering the
same rightly is called right.'

John Donne

Another famous churchman, perhaps better known as a poet (see
page 75), was John Donne (1572-1631). After spending his youth
and early manhood at the Inns of Court, and his middle years in
seclusion from public life (see Biographical Glossary), Donne took holy
orders in 1615. Although brought up as a Catholic, he converted to
the Church of England and was appointed Dean of St Paul's
Cathedral in 1621. He had written love poetry and satire in his youth,
and he turned his verbal dexterity and wit to good account in his
sermons, which reportedly drove their hearers to extremes of
emotion. He was taken ill in 1623, and used the occasion to write a
series of meditations on mortality which he called *Devotions upon
Emergent Occasions* (1624) from which the following well-known
passage comes:

> 'No man is an island, entire of itself; every man is a
> piece of the continent, a part of the main; if a clod be
> washed away by the sea, Europe is the less, as well
> as if a promontory were, as well as if a manor of thy
> friends, or of thine own were; any man's death
> diminishes me, because I am involved in mankind;
> and therefore never send to know for whom the bell
> tolls; it tolls for thee.'

During his final illness in 1631, he preached his last sermon
dressed in his death shroud (see illustration on page 57). The
occasion was considered to be Donne's preaching of his own funeral
sermon, and the text was printed as a pamphlet entitled 'Death's
Duel', with an engraving of Donne in his shroud on the cover.

The Classics and education

Although the greatest authors of the English Renaissance are best
known for their work in the forms of drama and verse, much of the
thinking and philosophy that underpinned their writing was
presented in prose. Classical and Continental authors were an
important source of ideas, and the delay between the start of the
Renaissance on the Continent and in England meant that English
writers were able to make good use of earlier authorities, either in
the original language or in translation. The rediscovery of learning
and the means of increasing knowledge in the Renaissance
brought with them a fresh approach to education. The humanist

line of thought was that an educated populace could interpret Scripture for themselves, could absorb the wisdom of the Classics and conduct themselves in an enlightened way in their daily dealings with their neighbors.

The work of Greek and Latin writers was the starting point of Renaissance education, and of these Cicero was the most revered for the clarity and orderliness of his rhetorical style, which, it was held, was a reflection of the honesty and integrity of his personal life. Latin was still the first language in the mid-16th century among educated people. For example, the French essayist and politician Michel de Montaigne (1533-92) spoke only Latin until he was six (when he learned French), and *In Praise of Folly* by Erasmus and *Utopia* by Sir Thomas More were both written, as a matter of course, in Latin.

The scholar John Colet (*c.*1467-1519), who had a significant influence on both Erasmus and More, founded St Paul's School in London in 1510. The statutes of the school included Colet's 'mission statement' for the education of the pupils:

> 'I would there were always taught good literature, both
> Latin and Greek, and good authors such as have the
> very Roman eloquence joined with wisdom, specially
> Christian authors that wrote their wisdom with clean
> and chaste Latin, other in verse or in prose; for my
> intent is by this school specially to increase
> knowledge and worshipping of God and Our Lord
> Christ Jesu and good Christian life and manners in the
> children... All barbary, all corruption, all Latin
> adulterate which ignorant blind fools brought into this
> world, and with that same hath disdained and
> poisoned the old Latin speech and the very Roman
> tongue which in the time of Tully [Cicero] and Sallust
> and Virgil and Terence was used... I say that filthiness
> and all such abusion which more rather may be called
> blotterature than literature, I utterly abanish and
> exclude out of this school.'

Although Colet was concerned to educate his pupils in a Christian manner, many of his preferred authors were of course 'pagan'. The humanist tradition embraced the sense of there being relative, rather than absolute, cultural values; enlightened teachers could present the differences between the Classical age and the Christian present without having to reinforce the superiority of the Christian age – there was, after all, an ever-increasing variety of Christian churches in Europe by the middle of the century, which gave the lie to the notion of a single faith.

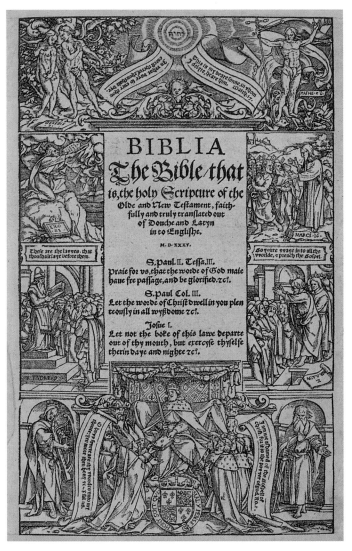

Hans Holbein the Younger, title page of Coverdale's Bible (1535)

Miles Coverdale printed the first complete English translation of the Bible in Zurich in 1535. Coverdale relied on the Vulgate (see page 51) and Martin Luther's German translation of the New Testament – the title page describes it as 'faithfully and truly translated out of Douche ['Deutsch': German] and Latyn'. Although it was not an authorized translation, Holbein gives the impression of official approval through the representation of Henry delivering the Bible to the bishops kneeling before him. Old and New Testament sayings and scenes are balanced against each other on either side of the design.

Nicholas Stone, *John Donne in his shroud*, sculpture in St Paul's Cathedral (1631-2)

During his last illness, Donne commissioned a portrait of himself in his winding-sheet, or funeral shroud. The picture was placed by his bedside and he used it to meditate upon mortality until he died. His friend Henry King arranged for an effigy in white marble to be made from the portrait, by Nicholas Stone, the greatest sculptor and mason of the time, and it was erected in St Paul's Cathedral. The effigy was one of the few artifacts to survive the destruction of the cathedral in the Great Fire of 1666, and still stands in Wren's building today.

Grammar schools also played an important part in spreading the influence of Greek and Latin authors within English culture, both in the original languages and in translations. They were founded by successive monarchs from Henry VI onwards, as well as by guilds and individual philanthropists such as Colet. The work of Shakespeare (who probably attended the grammar school at Stratford) contains references to Arthur Golding's translation of Ovid's *Metamorphoses* (1565), for example, and his Roman plays owe much to Sir Thomas North's translation (from a French version by Jacques Amyot) of Plutarch's *Lives* (1579). Plutarch (c.AD46-c.119) was a Greek writer who wrote a series of *Parallel Lives* of Greek and Roman heroes which remained a popular source of Classical history from their publication right through to the Renaissance.

Education was the subject of *The Scholemaster* (printed in 1570) by the scholar Roger Ascham (1515-68), who wrote in an earlier book, *Toxophilus* (1545), that he was writing 'Englishe matter in the Englishe tongue for Englishe men'. Although *The Scholemaster* is concerned with the teaching of the Classics to develop a love of harmony and order in the young, its clear English and its underlying humanist message that education is a civilizing force demonstrate the developing place of English as a natural successor to Latin as the language of rhetoric and debate. Ascham wrote in *The Scholemaster*:

'I do gladly agree with all good schoolmasters in

—— SHAKESPEARE'S BORROWING ——

Shakespeare was unconcerned about borrowing the actual expression as well as ideas from his literary sources. Some passages, such as the following description of Cleopatra in her barge on the way to meet Antony, from Antony and Cleopatra, *suggest that he must have worked with North's translation of Plutarch open in front of him:*

Shakespeare:
'The barge she sat in, like a burnished throne
Burned on the water. The poop was beaten gold;
Purple the sails, and so perfumèd that
The winds were love-sick with them. The oars were silver,
Which to the tune of flutes kept stroke, and made
The water which they beat to follow faster,
As amorous of their strokes. For her own person,
It beggared all description. She did lie
In her pavilion — cloth of gold, of tissue —
O'er-picturing that Venus where we see
The fancy outwork nature. On each side her
Stood pretty dimpled boys, like smiling Cupids,
With divers-coloured fans whose wind did seem
To glow the delicate cheeks which they did cool,
And what they undid did'

North's translation of Plutarch's Lives:
'She disdained to set forward otherwise but to take her barge in the river of Cydnus, the poop whereof was of gold, the sails of purple, and the oars of silver, which kept stroke in rowing after the sound of music of flutes, hautboys, citterns, viols, and such other instruments as they played upon in the barge. And now for the person of herself: she was laid under a pavilion of cloth of gold of tissue, apparelled and attired like the goddess Venus commonly drawn in picture, and hard by her, on either hand of her, pretty fair boys apparelled as painters do set forth god Cupid, with little fans in their hands with the which they fanned wind upon her.'

these points: to have children brought to good perfectness in learning, to all honesty in manners, to have all faults rightly amended, to have every vice severely corrected; but for the order and way that leadeth rightly to these points, we somewhat differ. For commonly many schoolmasters, some as I have seen, moe as I have heard tell, be of so crooked a nature as, when they meet with a hard-witted scholar, they rather break him than bow him, rather mar him than mend him. For when the schoolmaster is angry with some other matter, then he will soonest fall to beat his scholar; and though he himself should be punished for his folly, yet must he beat some scholar for his pleasure.'

Statesmanship and manners

The Classics, and the wider humanist education of which they were a part, were also considered important in instilling a sense of civic responsibility in individual members of society. Although the argument persisted in some quarters that teaching people to read and write would lead only to dissatisfaction and social unrest, the development of an educated population was one of the goals of the Protestant Tudor monarchs, who were themselves cultured and well-educated. There was no shortage of books and treatises on the subject of how monarchs should rule, and on how the populace should accept that rule.

Erasmus himself wrote a handbook for would-be rulers (*Institutio Christiani Principis* 'The Education of a Christian Prince', 1516), which Sir Thomas Elyot (c.1490-1546) acknowledged as a source for his influential treatise *The Book named the Governor* (1531). Elyot was a contemporary and friend of Sir Thomas More and John Colet, and in his book he aimed to provide English readers with a model of the education of the ideal Renaissance ruler. He thought that the relationship between the monarch and the court was particularly important: the nobility had a duty to advise the monarch, who had a reciprocal duty to heed good counsel.

Behind Elyot's manual of good government lurked an unspoken tension between two opposing views: that a monarch enjoyed a sacred right to rule as he or she wished, and that a monarch was constrained by obligations to his or her subjects. The Reformation led to the rise of the belief among some Protestant groups that God was the only authority in secular life as well as in matters of faith. This led to increasing friction between the court and the Puritans, which came to a head in the English Civil War. The beginnings of this conflict between monarch and people can be found in the 16th century in such diverse texts as Hooker's *Laws of Ecclesiastical*

He was a courtier, statesman, soldier and poet, who wrote an influential sonnet sequence, *Astrophel and Stella*; a famous piece of criticism, *The Defence of Poesie*; and the greatest Elizabethan prose romance, *The Arcadia*. Educated at Shrewsbury and Oxford, he entered the life of the court in 1576 as ambassador to the German emperor, and was subsequently Member of Parliament for Kent and appointed in 1585 as Master of the Ordnance, the office that provided supplies to the army. At the end of that year Elizabeth sent an expedition to the Netherlands under the command of the Earl of Leicester to support the Dutch in their fight for independence from Spanish rule. Sidney was made governor of the town of Flushing, and spent 11 months trying to maintain morale among his badly-equipped and unmotivated troops. He was involved in an action against the Spanish at Zutphen, in Flanders, in September 1586, and died from wounds received there, allegedly giving a cup of water in his last hours to a dying soldier with the words "Thy need is greater than mine."

A second major contribution to English letters, *The Defence of Poesie* (printed 1595, and also known by its alternative title, *An Apologie for Poetry*) set out to defend imaginative writing against an attack on drama by the Puritan, Stephen Gosson, and against claims that it was an inferior art form because it merely copied nature, that literature in general was subversive against the state, and that poetry was essentially misguided and self-centered. The key to his argument was that (good) poetry imitates a Platonic ideal (see page 8), hinting at how things should be, as opposed to the inadequacy of the real world. Sidney's third great work was *The Arcadia* (published 1591), a long prose romance that drew on the traditions of Greek and Italian narratives. He worked on it from 1577 to 1584 and left it in two separate versions at his death. His sister, the Countess of Pembroke, published a final version that incorporated many of her own emendations to Sidney's text, known as *The Countess of Pembroke's Arcadia* (1593). Characteristically, Sidney described the work (180,000 words long) in a letter to his sister, printed as the preface to the work, as 'this idle work of mine, which, I fear, like the spider's web, will be thought fitter to be swept away than worn to any other purpose'. A fine example of *sprezzatura*, indeed.

— SIR FRANCIS BACON —

Another man with all-round talent was Sir Francis Bacon (1561-1626). He started his career as a lawyer, subsequently served as a member of Parliament for a variety of constituencies, and under the reign of James I rose to become Lord Chancellor until he was forced from office for accepting bribes while a judge. Bacon wrote a great number of essays, a form pioneered by Michel de Montaigne (see page 56), on a wide range of subjects including law, history, education, health, horticulture, politics and government, religion and colonialism. Although not scientifically trained, he was interested in the language and method of deduction and observation; he retained William Harvey (see page 12) as his private physician. Harvey was himself a keen practitioner of empirical investigation (based on the results of experiment and observation rather than deduction from general principles) in his research on the circulatory system.

John de Critz the Elder,
Lucy Harington, Countess of Bedford (1606)

Lucy Harington, Countess of Bedford, was the sister of Sir John Harington, author of one of the most influential of Elizabethan translations, Ariosto's *Orlando Furioso* (1591). She was, along with Mary Sidney, Countess of Pembroke (see page 62), among the most important patrons of poetry in the early 17th century. She was a poet herself, and encouraged others including John Donne and Ben Jonson. She is seen here in a masque costume designed by Inigo Jones, who was the favored designer of James I's court.

Travel, journalism and entertainment

The 16th-century book trade was prolific: a great range of subjects such as health and herbal medicine, geography and travel, cookery and husbandry, geometry and math were all available. Certain kinds of writing were perceived as having less commercial value. At the bottom of the heap were broadsheets or broadside ballads. These were verses written on a topical subject such as politics, war, religion or what would today be called 'human interest', illustrated with woodcut pictures and printed on one side of a single folio sheet.

An early form of journalism also existed in the form of pamphlets, usually written in defense of current religious or political debate and designed to stir up controversy. Among the most infamous pamphlets were those written by 'Martin Marprelate', a pseudonym for a Puritan writer or writers who attacked the notion of a church governed by bishops in a series of pamphlets published in 1588-9 (the 'Marprelate controversy'). Another popular series were the 'cony-catching' ('cony' was a slang term for a dupe), pamphlets written in the early 1590s by Robert Greene and Thomas Dekker, describing the London underworld in all its lurid forms from the point of view of a trickster, or 'cony-catcher'. Thomas Nashe conducted a lengthy satirical battle for almost a decade against his rival, the scholar Gabriel Harvey (c.1550-1631) through pamphlets with titles such as *Have with You to Saffron Walden* (1596). This pamphlet battle was eventually brought to an end through the intervention of the Archbishop of Canterbury. Pamphlets, along with playscripts and poetry, were usually printed by licensed printers, but were not considered a particularly prestigious sector of the market.

The novel did not develop as a major literary form until the 18th century, but its ancestry can be traced back through the fictional travel writing of Daniel Defoe (*Robinson Crusoe,* 1719) and Jonathan Swift (*Gulliver's Travels,* 1726) to the prose fiction of the Elizabethan and Jacobean period and More's *Utopia.* Travel writing existed as a lively genre in itself, dating back to the fictional *Travels of Sir John Mandeville* (c.1357) by an anonymous author. In the second half of the 16th century curiosity about the foreign lands that were being exploited by the European powers, and about the Continent itself, led to a variety of literature on the subject. The most widely-read travel writer was Richard Hakluyt (1552-1616), a geographer who spent his life promoting exploration, colonization, navigation and mapmaking. He was involved in the voyages of Sir Humphrey Gilbert and Sir Martin Frobisher (see page 14) and the colonization of Virginia (founded at Jamestown in 1607). As well as translations of a number of European books on exploration, Hakluyt published a substantial record of English seafaring achievements called *Principal Navigations, Voyages and Discoveries of the English Nation* (first published in 1589 and substantially revised in 1598), designed to show how his country could match the discoveries of Spain and Portugal.

Other examples of travel literature include Sir Walter Raleigh's *Report of the Fight about the Azores* (1591) and *The Discovery of the Large, Rich and Beautiful Empire of Guiana* (1596); Captain John Smith's history of the founding of Virginia, and *Coryate's Crudities* (1611), an account of Thomas Coryat's travels in Europe.

A genre allied to travel writing was the picaresque. In a strict sense it tells of the exploits of a servant (from the Spanish *picaró*) who enjoys a series of escapades in the service of several masters. More generally, it was the novelistic equivalent of the modern-day road movie, consisting of several largely unrelated episodes held together by the presence of a central character. *Don Quixote* (1605) by the Spanish author Miguel de Cervantes (1547-1616) is the most well-known example of this genre, which originated in Spain. There is, however, an early English example, Thomas Nashe's *The Unfortunate Traveller* (1594). Nashe was one of the 'university wits' (see page 26) and a truly idiosyncratic writer. He courted controversy and was imprisoned and subsequently banished from London for his part in the writing of *The Isle of Dogs*, a play highly critical of government corruption (see page 42). *The Unfortunate Traveller* tells the story of Jack Wilton, a 'certain kind of an appendix or page' in the army in Europe at the time of Henry VIII, who is embroiled in a succession of adventures across the Continent. In Wittenberg, for example, Wilton observes an entertainment for the Duke of Saxony:

> 'A bursten-belly inkhorn orator called Vanderhulke, they picked out to present him with an oration, one that had a sulphurous big swollen large face like a Saracen, eyes like two Kentish oysters, a mouth that opened as wide every time he spake, as one of those old knit trap doors, a beard as though it had been made of a bird's nest plucked in pieces, which consisteth of straw, hair and dirt mixed together. He was apparelled in black leather new liquored [lubricated], & a short gown without any gathering in the back, faced before and behind with a boisterous bearskin, and a red nightcap on his head.'

The description has an extra resonance since it is likely to be a caricature of Nashe's rival, Gabriel Harvey (see page 64).

Thomas Deloney (*c.*1543-1600), a silk-weaver and ballad-maker, wrote fiction in the same vein, using his experiences as an artisan as the basis for such tales as *Jack of Newbury* (1597), relating the adventures of a broadcloth weaver, or *The Gentle Craft* (1597), which is a celebration of the shoemakers' company and a source for Thomas Dekker's play *The Shoemaker's Holiday* (see page 33). Dekker was himself a vigorous prose writer in the early 1600s. He wrote a number of pamphlets about contemporary issues: *The Wonderfull Yeare* (1603) on the plague in London (see page 75); *The Bellman of London* (1608) about the urban underworld; and *The Gull's Horn Book* [handbook] (1609), a satirical view of the fashionable theatre scene of his day.

A very different kind of prose could be found in the work of Thomas Lodge and John Lyly (1554-1606). Another of the 'university wits', Lodge wrote popular pamphlets such as *A Defence of Plays or Wits Miserie* (1580*)*, but he was best known as a translator of French and Italian literature. On a buccaneering expedition to the Canary Islands in 1588 he wrote *Rosalynde: Euphues Golden Legacie*, which Shakespeare used as the source for the plot of *As You Like It* (c.1599). The use of Euphues in the title of *Rosalynde* refers to the prose romance by John Lyly called *Euphues, or the Anatomy of Wit* (1578). Lyly's story has little plot, but much style, and its artificiality and elegantly ornate language was much imitated for the remainder of the century. The term 'euphuism', meaning a way of writing that involves affected and overwrought linguistic effect, was coined by Gabriel Harvey in 1593. The following extract gives an example of Lyly's style:

> '"Nay Lucilla," said he, "my harvest shall cease, seeing others have reaped my corn, as for angling for the fish that is already caught, that were but mere folly. But in my mind if you be a fish you are either an eel which as soon as one hath hold of her tail, will slip out of his hand, or else a minnow which will be nibbling at every bait but never biting: But what fish so ever you be you have made both me and Philautus to swallow a gudgeon... and therefore farewell Lucilla, the most inconstant that ever was nursed in Naples, farewell Naples the most cursed town in all Italy, and women all farewell."'

5. POETRY

Compared to drama or prose, poetry in some of its forms was a more intimate, less public form of writing in the Renaissance. A number of the 16th- and 17th-century poets who are most widely read today, including Sir Philip Sidney, John Donne and George Herbert, did not publish their work during their lifetimes, although their poetry was circulated in manuscript among their friends and acquaintances.

Tudor origins

One reason for the unwillingness to publish was the social stigma of a gentleman writing for money and the relatively minor status afforded to poetry as a form of writing. Poetry was in many ways regarded as a 'courtly' accomplishment, and so outside the commercial mainstream that sustained the livelihood of dramatists, lawyers and theologians. This was a tradition going back to Geoffrey Chaucer (c.1340-1400), whose poetry was written to be read by and to a courtly audience familiar with the various styles, traditions and conventions on which he drew, and to John Skelton at the court of Henry VIII (see page 21). The growing commercialization of poetry can be seen in the development of copyright law (see box).

The Court

Wyatt and Surrey

The two men who are credited with the creation of a distinctive English voice in Renaissance poetry – Henry Howard, Earl of Surrey and Sir Thomas Wyatt – were both at the forefront of the politics of their day. Wyatt (1503-42) was a popular member of the court of Henry VIII, and, like Sir Philip Sidney, a Renaissance courtier who was renowned as a linguist, scholar, astronomer and musician. He was well-regarded as a diplomat, too, serving in France and Spain. It is likely that he was the lover of Anne Boleyn before Henry's eye fell on her, and he was imprisoned in the Tower of London twice, managing on both occasions to escape execution. The Earl of Surrey (1517-47) was

—— COPYRIGHT AND MONOPOLIES——

The earliest law of copyright, which protects an author's right to sell and publish his or her own work, was not passed until the reign of Queen Anne, in 1709. Before that time, an author could not prevent a printer or publisher from selling his or her work, and there was no guarantee either of the accuracy of the text, or of any payment for the author as a result of its publication. The printing and bookselling industry was growing fast and was tightly regulated, which meant that there were good profits to be made by those in the business. Printing and selling books was controlled by the Stationers' Company, the regulatory guild incorporated by royal charter in 1557, which was granted the power to impose fines, control promotion within the craft and take action against unlicensed publishers. Queen Mary's prime motive in granting the charter was to use the Company to suppress religious nonconformity, but it also exercised a monopoly over a wide range of various kinds of books such as dictionaries, music books, grammars, bibles and legal publications. Legislation passed in 1586 restricted presses to London and the two university towns of Cambridge and Oxford. The members of the Company were required to keep records of every book they produced, which have proved very valuable to scholars tracing the literature of the period.

even closer to the heart of the court. He was the eldest son of the Duke of Norfolk, the senior nobleman in the country, and cousin to Catherine Howard, Henry VIII's fourth wife. Although he was a cultured man and a distinguished soldier, he became embroiled in the political jostling that accompanied the closing stages of the reign of Henry VIII: the Howards were rivals of the Seymour family (Jane Seymour was Henry's third wife and mother of his only son, the future Edward VI), and Surrey and his father were arrested in 1546 on a false charge of treason. Surrey was executed, the last person to be so treated by Henry VIII, and his father escaped only as a result of the king's death.

The innovation that Wyatt and Surrey brought to English poetry was the introduction of Continental – specifically Italian – forms and styles. Their model was the medieval Italian scholar and poet Petrarch (1304-74), whose poetry was often written in sonnet form (see box). Petrarch's writing was also characterized by motifs of change and restlessness (which Edmund Spenser was to call 'mutabilitie' in a section at the end of *The Faerie Queene*), and often focused on the poet's emotions as a result of his unfulfilled love for his beloved, known only as Laura. In some cases the poetry of both Wyatt and Surrey was a close translation of Petrarch's work, in others it was much freer, evoking the mood and idiom, but communicating their own emotion and experience. Their imitation and adaptation of the sonnet form to suit the metrical patterns of the English language was an important factor in the direction of English poetry. The intricate rhyme scheme of the sonnet, the metrical demands of 14 lines of iambic pentameter, and the separation into sections of eight and six lines made the art of composition more demanding than it had been with the looser forms of the past, presenting a formal challenge to the sophisticated urbane courtiers who admired and succeeded Wyatt and Surrey. The work of both men was first printed in an anthology, Tottell's *Miscellany*, published in 1557.

Gloriana

While the court of Henry VIII was the milieu of the first poetry of the English Renaissance, it was the court of Elizabeth I that provided the setting for the next flourishing of poetry. Edmund Spenser (c.1552-99) planned a large-scale poem in 12 books which would put English at the forefront of European literature and develop a moral theme for its readers. His poem, *The Faerie Queene* (1590-6), looked back to the medieval tradition of allegorical writing (see Glossary of Terms) and to the legends of King Arthur and his knights. The six books that Spenser completed before his death record the exploits of six knights, including the Red Cross Knight, St George, and a female knight called Britomart. But

— THE SONNET —

A sonnet is a poem consisting of 14 lines. Its use in English originated with the translations and adaptations by Wyatt and Surrey of the Italian sonnets of Petrarch, and it traditionally took love as its subject. In its Italian form (known as the 'Petrarchan') it divides into an eight-line stanza (the 'octave') and a six line stanza (the 'sestet'). The octave has a rhyme scheme of abba abba, *the sestet usually either* cdcdcd *or* cdecde. *In its English form the lines consist of ten syllables, typically in iambic pentameter (see Glossary of Terms). Because there were fewer rhymes for words in English than in Italian, a rhyme pattern that allowed greater freedom for the poet became characteristic of the English sonnet:* abab cdcd efef gg. *This had the effect of rearranging the structure of the poem into three four-line stanzas ('quatrains') and a final rhyming couplet. In the Petrarchan model, the sestet can provide a contrast to the theme presented in the octave, (the moment at which the thought pattern changes direction is called the* volta, *meaning 'turn') but in the English pattern (often called 'Shakespearean') the three quatrains often reinforce the same idea, which is affirmed or contradicted in the closing couplet. Shakespeare's Sonnet 30 illustrates this pattern well:*

When *to the sessions of sweet silent thought*
I summon up remembrance of things past,
I sigh the lack of many a thing I sought,
And with old woes new wail my dear time's waste;
Then *can I drown an eye (unused to flow)*
For precious friends hid in death's dateless night,
And weep afresh love's long-since cancelled woe,
And moan th'expense of many a vanished sight;
Then *can I grieve at grievances foregone,*
And heavily from woe to woe tell o'er
The sad account of fore-bemoanèd moan,
Which I new pay as if not paid before.
    But *if the while I think on thee (dear friend)*
    All losses are restored and sorrows end.

Sir Philip Sidney wrote the sonnet sequence Astrophel and Stella *to record his frustrated feelings of love for Penelope Devereux. The following sonnet (No. 71 in the sequence) follows the strict form of the Petrarchan rhyme scheme:*

Who will in fairest book of nature know	*a*
How virtue may best lodged in beauty be,	*b*
Let him but learn of love to read in thee,	*b*
Stella, those fair lines which true goodness show.	*a*
There shall he find all vices' overthrow,	*a*
Not by rude force, but sweetest sovereignty	*b*
Of reason, from whose light those night-birds fly,	*b*
That inward sun in thine eyes shineth so.	*a*
And, not content to be perfection's heir	*c*
Thyself, dost strive all minds that way to move,	*d*
Who mark in thee what is in thee most fair;	*c*
So while thy beauty draws the heart to love,	*d*
As fast thy virtue bends that love to good.	*e*
But ah, desire still cries, 'Give me some food!'	*e*

Spenser avoided creating an entirely idealized world by linking his fairy world to the world of Elizabeth's court: she was the Faerie Queene, also known as Gloriana, and the dangers confronting her knights were the contemporary issues confronting England, such as the threat from Rome and the colonization of Ireland. In the prefatory letter to Sir Walter Raleigh, Spenser wrote:

> 'In that Faery Queene I meane glory in my generall intention, but in my particular I conceive the most excellent and glorious person of our soveraine the Queene, and her kingdome in Faery land. And yet, in some places els, I doe otherwise shadow [hint at] her.'

The jousting and feats of arms that Gloriana's knights undertake in the poem were also mirrored in the life of Elizabeth's court. The queen was extremely canny in building up a mystique around her unmarried status, and cultivated images of herself as the Virgin Queen, wedded to her nation and able to bestow her favor on all suitors. She had her favorites – the Earl of Leicester, the Earl of Essex, Sir Walter Raleigh – but enjoyed presiding over a court where virtue, art and prowess all had their place. The anniversary of her accession to the throne, 17 November, was celebrated with elaborate tournaments in mock medieval fancy dress, creating a modern world of pageantry and chivalry to rival the best of mythological traditions. A visiting German, Lupold von Wedel, watched the tilts of 1584:

> 'During the whole time of the tournament all those who wished to fight entered the list by pairs, the trumpets being blown at the time, and other musical instruments... There were some who showed very good horsemanship and were also in fine attire. The manner of the combat each had settled before entering the lists. When a gentleman with his servants approached the barrier, on horseback or in a carriage, he stopped at the foot of the staircase leading to the queen's room, while one of his servants in pompous attire of a special pattern mounted the steps and addressed the queen in well-composed verses or with a ludicrous speech, making her and her ladies laugh.'

Elizabeth's reign as the Fairy Queen was celebrated in many other forms besides poetry. A number of the most famous portraits of Elizabeth represent her in various allegorical ways: as the victor of the Armada (see illustration page 9); as Cynthia, goddess of the Moon; holding an ermine, which symbolizes chastity; or as the

Nicholas Hilliard,
Young Man amongst Roses (c.1587)

Nicholas Hilliard (1547-1619) was a goldsmith, a jeweler, and a painter of miniatures who painted Queen Elizabeth and many members of her court. This portrait may be of Robert Devereux, 2nd Earl of Essex, one of Elizabeth's favorites. As with the Armada portrait of Elizabeth (see page 9), this painting contains significant iconographic detail: black and white were the personal colors of Elizabeth, while the five-petalled white eglantine rose was closely associated with the queen. The portrait could represent a courtier signalling his love for Elizabeth, or it could be simply a picture of a lovesick, romantic young man.

empress of the world. She was also widely commemorated in music, particularly in madrigals (see box). A significant collection of madrigals was *The Triumphs of Oriana*, edited and published in 1601 by Thomas Morley. Each of the settings is a celebration, in pastoral form, of the reign of Queen Elizabeth, and each ends with the words 'Long live fair Oriana'. This name, often used in pastoral poetry to refer to the queen, demonstrates that the link between the queen and the pastoral tradition (see page 77) promoted in Spenser's poem was still strong. However, *The Triumphs of Oriana* was published in the year of the Earl of Essex's rebellion (an unsuccessful popular revolt in London led by the Queen's former favorite), when Elizabeth was in decline, and the myth of Gloriana was fading fast.

While serving in Ireland in the late 1580s (see page 15) Spenser built up a strong rapport with Sir Walter Raleigh, who owned neighboring estates near Cork. Raleigh persuaded Spenser to present *The Faerie Queene* personally to Elizabeth: the poem is prefaced with a letter to Raleigh setting out the poet's intentions in writing it, which were 'to fashion a gentleman or noble person in virtuous and gentle discipline'. Raleigh himself had written allegorical poems in honor of the queen, unpublished in his lifetime. In 'Ocean's Love to Cynthia', he plays on the image of Elizabeth as the goddess of the Moon and on his own role as the ocean: 'Walter' was pronounced 'water'. One of his finest poems, 'As you came from the holy land', also alludes to Elizabeth, implying an association with the Virgin Mary in its references to the Shrine of the Virgin at Walsingham in Norfolk, which was an important center of pilgrimage before the Dissolution of the Monasteries under Henry VIII (see page 7):

—— THE MADRIGAL AND —— ### THE LUTE SONG

The madrigal was a secular setting of lyric poetry for unaccompanied voices singing in parts. It reached the height of its popularity in Italy in the second half of the 16th century in the work of composers such as Orlande de Lassus, Giovanni Pierluigi da Palestrina and Claudio Monteverdi.

The form reached England by about 1570, and it quickly developed its own character. There was a large quantity of lyric poetry in circulation and a flourishing tradition of music-making within the home as well as in churches. The growth of the madrigal as a popular musical form coincided with the arrival of pastoral art and literature, and the simplicity of pastoral lent itself naturally to such a musical setting. A high proportion of English madrigal texts are pastoral poems, often fairly conventional in character, but the musical settings are usually very sympathetic to the words and the mood of the poetry. Each musical part was printed separately, and although written primarily for unaccompanied voices, madrigals could be performed by voices or viols — stringed instruments of the same family as the violin and cello — in any available combination. One of the characteristics of the madrigal is a refrain sung to the syllables fa-la, which was used as a nickname for the genre. The leading composers of the form were Thomas Morley (1557-1602), Thomas Weelkes (c.1575-1623) and John Wilbye (1574-1628).

Solo songs, called 'ayres', were usually accompanied by a consort of viols or by the lute, and came into fashion at the turn of the century as madrigals declined in popularity. Often printed in folio volumes, the music was set out so that the performers could read their parts from the same page sitting on three sides of a table. John Dowland (1562-1626) and Thomas Campion (1567-1620) were the foremost composers of lute songs, Campion often setting his own lyric poetry. Songs such as 'Weep you no more sad fountains' or 'There is a garden in her face' are fine examples of the genre.

'As you came from the holy land
Of Walsinghame,
Met you not with my true love
By the way as you came?

How shall I know your true love,
That have met many one,
As I went to the holy land,
That have come, that have gone?

She is neither white nor brown,
But as the heavens fair;
There is none hath a form so divine
In the earth or the air.

Such a one did I meet, good sir,
Such an angelic face,
Who like a queen, like a nymph, did appear
By her gait, by her grace.

She hath left me here all alone,
All alone, as unknown,
Who sometimes did me lead with herself,
And me loved as her own.'

Weddings

Dynastic marriages among the nobility were common during the
period, and wedding ceremonies were often accompanied by lavish
entertainments. In Elizabeth's time, plays were written to mark
such occasions; in James I's reign, the masque became the
preferred dramatic form. Authors such as Ben Jonson and Thomas
Campion (1567-1620) wrote masques to represent the allegorical
virtues or qualities of the married couple. This practice was also
seen within drama itself: in Shakespeare's *The Tempest* Prospero
commands a betrothal masque for Miranda and Ferdinand.

Poetry was also used to celebrate matrimony, and two of
Spenser's better-known shorter poems are wedding hymns.
Epithalamion, published at the end of his sonnet sequence
Amoretti, commemorates his own wedding to Elizabeth Boyle in
1594, while *Prothalamion* marks the double wedding of Lady
Elizabeth and Lady Katherine Somerset, daughters of the Earl of
Worcester, in 1596. *Prothalamion* is primarily set in the pastoral
mode (see page 77), with the two brides are allegorized as swans.
The River Thames – captured in the refrain 'Sweet Thames, run
softly till I end my song' – links the idealized world of the
countryside to the city of London:

'merry London, my most kindly Nurse,
That to me gave this Life's first native source,
Though from another place I take my name,
An house of ancient fame:
There when they came, whereas those bricky towers
The which on Thames' broad agèd back do ride,
Where now the studious Lawyers have their bowers,
There whilom wont the Templar Knights to bide,
Till they decayed through pride:
Next whereunto there stands a stately place,
Where oft I gained gifts and goodly grace
Of that great Lord, which therein wont to dwell,
Whose want too well now feels my friendless case;'

The reference to the 'stately place' belonging to the 'great Lord' is to Essex House, once the property of the Earl of Leicester in whose household Spenser had been employed, and where the Worcester nuptials took place. In the 16th century, there was a mile of palaces between Whitehall and the City of London bearing the names of their owners, including Northumberland House, York House, the Savoy Palace, Somerset House, Arundel House and Essex House. None survives in its original form, but the names have survived to the present.

——— ROYAL PALACES ———

In the 16th century the distinction still existed between the City of London, governed by the Corporation of London since medieval times and associated with trade and finance, and the City of Westminster, where the Palace of Westminster and the Abbey symbolized royalty and political power. Elizabeth and James I were able to choose from a variety of royal residences in London: the Tower, which was the only palace within the City, and Whitehall, St James's and Westminster palaces in the city of Westminster. Beyond London the royal palaces included Windsor Castle in Berkshire; Hampton Court (built by Henry VIII's Lord Chancellor, Cardinal Wolsey, and then given by Wolsey to the king when he fell from grace); Hatfield House in Hertfordshire; Richmond Palace in Surrey; and Greenwich Palace on the banks of the Thames in north Kent. The oldest surviving part of Greenwich Palace is the Queen's House, designed by Inigo Jones in 1616 for Anne of Denmark, wife of James I. The Queen's House is notable for being the first building in England built in the neo-Classical style. Henry VIII's palace of Nonsuch in Surrey was the most extravagant and elaborate of all the royal palaces, but it was demolished in about 1670, surviving only in contemporary drawings and first-hand accounts by diarists such as Samel Pepys (1633-1703) and John Evelyn (1620-1706).

The favorite country residence of James I was Theobalds in Hertfordshire. The house was built by William Cecil, Lord Burghley in the 1560s and '70s as a private house. When James visited the palace in 1607 he was so taken with it that he persuaded Robert Cecil, who had inherited it from his father, to exchange it for Hatfield. Such a request could not comfortably be refused, and James quickly made the place his own, encircling the estate with a brick wall nine and a half miles long. He died there in 1625; the palace was dismantled and fell into decay during the Commonwealth (1649-60).

The City

Plague

London was a rapidly expanding city. The population in 1580 was roughly 100,000; by 1600 it had doubled, and by 1650 it was 400,000. The City of London was still bounded by the medieval city walls, but over time it had incorporated suburbs outside the city walls such as Holborn, Clerkenwell and Moorfields as part of greater London. On the south side of the Thames, the Borough of Southwark was an important center as a result of its position at one end of London Bridge, the only crossing point by road over the river.

Overcrowding and lack of sanitation (most streets had an open sewer running down the middle) made London an unhealthy place, and the bubonic plague was a regular hazard of city life. Plague epidemics occurred, for example in 1570, 1592-4, 1603 and 1609. In the epidemic of 1603 about one-sixth of the city's population died within 12 months. Outbreaks of the plague had a major impact on the life of the city: anyone who could do so moved to the country. Thomas Dekker satirized this response in his pamphlet *The Wonderfull Yeare*, here addressing an imaginary well-to-do citizen: 'Thou art gotten safe out of the civil city, Calamity, to thy parks and palaces in the country, lading thy asses and thy mules with thy gold (thy god!), thy plate and thy jewels; and the fruits of thy womb thriftily growing up in but one son, him hast thou also rescued from the arrows of infection.'

The theatres were considered breeding grounds for the plague and were closed for extended periods during epidemics. The outbreak of 1609 may have had one positive consequence: although Shakespeare had possibly completed his *Sonnets* by 1599, they were not published until 1609—perhaps because the theatres had been intermittently closed from 1603 to 1604 and again from 1606 to 1610. Shakespeare's writing for the theatre was disrupted by these closures, and so he revised and published poetry written several years earlier in order to supplement his income.

City life

Like Edmund Spenser, John Donne (see page 55) tried to make his mark on the fringes of the court in London during the 1590s. A member of a Catholic family, Donne trained as a lawyer and then in the 1590s took part in the expeditions of the Earl of Essex to Cadiz and the Azores (see page 14). During his time in London's Inns of Court, Donne wrote a substantial number of poems which were circulated in manuscript but only published two years after his death, in 1633, under the title of *Songs and Sonets*. In these and other works Donne created a new and distinctive style of English poetry (later given the title 'Metaphysical' poetry) which was in marked contrast to

the polished and complimentary manner of Spenser and Sidney.
Whereas Spenser's London is an elegant and courtly city, Donne's
London is a vibrant and earthy place, as depicted in his Fourth Satire:

'My mind, neither with pride's itch, nor yet hath been
Poisoned with love to see or to be seen,
I had no suit there, nor no new suit to show,
Yet went to Court...
Therefore I suffered this: towards me did run
A thing more strange than on Nile's slime the sun
E'er bred; or all which into Noah's ark came;
A thing which would have posed Adam to name;
Stranger than seven antiquaries' studies,
Than Afric's monsters, Guiana's rarities...
He names me, and comes to me; I whisper 'God!
How have I sinned, that thy wrath's furious rod,
This fellow, chooseth me?'...
He knows who loves; whom; and who by poison
Hastes to an Office's reversion;
He knows who hath sold his land, and now doth beg
A licence, old iron, boots, shoes, and egg-
Shells to transport; shortly boys shall not play
At span-counter or blow-point but they pay
Toll to some courtier; and wiser than all us,
He knows what lady is not painted. Thus
He with home-meats tries me. I belch, spew, spit,
Look pale and sickly like a patient. Yet
He thrusts on more.'

The poetry of Donne and the drama of Ben Jonson in
particular (see page 30) give the reader a sense of the hot-house
atmosphere of London at the turn of the 16th century. Both
Elizabeth and James I sold off large tracts of property and
monopolies in order to finance their expensive foreign ventures
and the continuing attempts to colonize Ireland. The opportunity
to secure land or manufacturing and mining rights, or to colonize
territory in the New World, attracted various speculators to the
court and created an atmosphere of faction, intrigue and
corruption. Such a spectacle increasingly damaged the
relationship between the crown and the growing middle classes,
and was satirized by the poets and dramatists of the time.
By the end of the century many writers, such as Spenser,
Marlowe, Shakespeare and Jonson, who were born into
middle-class families and were beneficiaries of the Classical
education of the grammar schools (see page 58), were
coming to prominence and drew comparisons between the

ages of Elizabeth and James I and of Augustus and the early Roman emperors. Italian verse forms such as the sonnet stood alongside Classical forms such as the satire or the epigram (see Glossary of Terms), which gave a sharper perspective on social trends.

The Country

The passionate shepherd

Countering the depiction of urban extravagance by Donne and Jonson was the pastoral, which enjoyed considerable popularity during the second half of the 16th century. Pastoral has its roots in the *Idylls* of the Greek poet Theocritus (3rd century BC). Writing for a sophisticated and literate city-based readership, Theocritus created an idealized world – set in his native Sicily – populated by shepherds and nymphs, where the problems of real life did not exist. The 1st-century Latin poet Virgil imitated Theocritus in his Eclogues (verse dialogues between shepherds in a rural setting), using the Greek region of Arcadia as the mythical setting for his shepherds and shepherdesses. The evocation of a simple country life in the *Odes* of Horace, Virgil's contemporary, provided a further model for the Elizabethan poets, who saw the possibilities of linking Arcadian simplicity to the reign of Gloriana.

From the outset, pastoral poetry was an urban interpretation of rural life; the pastoral landscape was a literary invention, rather than a realistic description of country life, and the characters who populated it were equally artificial or stereotyped. In both its Classical and Renaissance forms, the pastoral looked back to a Golden Age in which people led simple lives unspoiled by the values that had made contemporary life unstable and imperfect. During Elizabethan times the Golden Age was used to represent a nostalgic view of the feudal past, before urban communities existed.

Pastoral was closely linked to satire: both were 'low' styles of writing (involving common people, as opposed, for example, to lyric poetry), and Renaissance writers

— RURAL LIFE —

The reality of rural life was far from idyllic. The end of the century saw consistently bad weather: the exceptionally cold, wet summers of 1594, 1595 and 1596 depressed agricultural wages and drove up the price of grain. The economic toll of many years of war against Spain and the restriction on trade in the city created by repeated plague epidemics only reinforced a sense of collective unrest as the century drew to a close and Elizabeth's health and energy waned. A glimpse of this troubled time appears in A Midsummer Night's Dream, *in the speech by Titania, the fairy queen, to her husband Oberon:*

'The ox hath therefore stretch'd his yoke in vain,
The ploughman lost his sweat, and the green corn
Hath rotted ere his youth attain'd a beard;
The fold stands empty in the drowned field,
And crows are fatted with the murrion flock;
The nine-men's morris is fill'd up with mud,
And the quaint mazes in the wanton green
For lack of tread are undistinguishable...
　　　　　　the spring, the summer,
The chiding autumn, angry winter, change
Their wonted liveries; and the mazed world,
By their increase, now knows not which is which.'

mistakenly believed that satire took its name from the mythical creatures, half-goat and half-man, which acted as the chorus in Greek drama (satyrs). Pastoral and satire each took a critical view of the city or the court, but expressed this view in different ways. If the poet cast himself in the role of the shepherd he could adopt the honest views and plain-speaking ways of the countryman which would gain the respect of his readers, and at the same time give the impression that he was removed from the society that he was judging in the poetry. Pastoral could also be invoked to eulogize (praise) the monarch or a patron – particularly if the poet was seeking a favor from the recipient.

The first major English imitation of the Classical model was Edmund Spenser's *The Shepheardes Calender* (1579). The poem took the form of 12 eclogues, one for each month of the year, and the characters represented real people: Spenser called himself Colin Clout, while his friend Gabriel Harvey was Hobbinol. 'April' was a hymn of praise to Elizabeth, while 'May' incorporated an animal fable, the fox and the kid, to illustrate the conflict between Protestant and Catholic values. The pastoral genre was widely adapted in all branches of literature: Sidney's prose pastoral *The Countess of Pembroke's Arcadia* and Shakespeare's comedy *As You Like It* are the best-known examples. The sense of a shared tradition is well illustrated by three poems by Marlowe, Raleigh and Donne. Marlowe's 'The Passionate Shepherd to his Love' (written c.1588) is a conventional pastoral love poem:

> 'Come live with me and be my love,
> And we will all the pleasures prove
> That valleys, groves, hills and fields,
> Woods, or steepy mountains yields.
>
> And we will sit upon the rocks,
> Seeing the shepherds feed their flocks
> By shallow rivers to whose falls
> Melodious birds sing madrigals...'

This poem was published in 1599, followed one year later by Sir Walter Raleigh's 'The Nymph's Reply to the Shepherd', which was designed to counter the youthful shepherd's optimism:

> 'If all the world and love were young
> And truth in every shepherd's tongue,
> These pretty pleasures might me move,
> To live with thee and be thy love.

Time drives the flock from field to fold,
When rivers rage and rocks grow cold,
And Philomel becometh dumb,
The rest complains of cares to come...'

By 1600 John Donne had also written a version of the poem, later given the title of 'the Bait', that offered an even more cynical slant on the original:

'Come live with me and be my love,
And we will some new pleasures prove,
Of golden sands and crystal brooks,
With silken lines and silver hooks.
There will the river whispering run,
Warmed by thy eyes more than the sun.
And there the enamoured fish will stay,
Begging themselves they may betray...'

Many noblemen and women lived full and untroubled lives beyond the intrigue and infighting of the court in the great houses of the Elizabethan period such as Hardwick Hall, Haddon Hall, Knole, Longleat and Montacute, and one strand of pastoral poetry celebrates the harmonious relationship between the estate and its master with an element of undisguised flattery: the poet was not in any way on a social par with his patron, and sometimes depended upon him for his livelihood. Penshurst Place was the seat of the Sidney family in Kent, and Ben Jonson's 'To Penshurst' (1616) records the hospitality and honesty of Lord Sidney (brother of Sir Philip) in his manor (see illustration page 81). Robert Herrick (1591-1674) wrote a celebratory poem to Sir Lewis Pemberton and his estate at Rushden in Northamptonshire. Andrew Marvell (1621-78), assistant to John Milton during the Commonwealth, worked as tutor to the daughter of Lord Fairfax, the successful general of the Parliamentary army in the English Civil War. Fairfax retired after the War and lived as a country gentleman at his house at Nun Appleton in Yorkshire and Marvell wrote a long poem entitled 'Upon Appleton House', describing the virtues and joys of the estate.

The Church

Divine poetry
The fourth main influence on Renaissance poetry, in addition to the court, the city and the country, was the Church. The two pre-eminent religious poets of the period were John Donne (see page 55) and George Herbert (1593-1633), neither of whom published their poetry during their lifetimes, since both viewed their work as primarily

meditative and personal. Herbert was brought up in a cultured family: his mother was a close friend of Donne, and his brother was created Baron Herbert of Cherbury for his political work during the reign of James I. After a period of time at Cambridge as university Orator, Herbert chose a life in the Church instead of a career at court. He sent a set of manuscript poems to his friend Nicholas Ferrar shortly before his death, leaving him with the choice whether to publish them or not. Ferrar did so, giving the volume the title *The Temple.* Using very simple language, Herbert wrote poems of intricate thought and structure, which immediately became popular. Many, such as 'Let all the world in every corner sing' and 'Teach me my God and King', were later set to music as hymns.

Herbert inspired other religious poets such as Richard Crashaw (1612-49), and Henry Vaughan (c.1621-95). Each had a very different set of beliefs from the others: Crashaw became a Roman Catholic in 1645, although he had already been strongly influenced by Italian poetry in his writing; Vaughan's commitment to the Church of England despite its unpopularity after the English Civil War is a strong feature of his poetry.

Robert Herrick (see page 79) was a clergyman, living at Dean Prior in Devon for most of his long career. He published his collected works as *Hesperides* and *Noble Numbers* in 1648; as a disciple of Ben Jonson he was primarily interested not in meditative verse but in Classical models and sentiments and much of his verse is in the form of elegies, satires and epigrams, as well as religious and love lyrics and pastorals. He is best known for the secular poem 'To the Virgins, to Make Much of Time', which begins: 'Gather ye rose-buds while ye may,/ Old Time is still a-flying.'

Other poets such as Andrew Marvell (see page 79) managed to communicate, in poetry which is less obviously devotional, a sense of the scope and mystery of the universe and its workings. In his poem 'On a Drop of Dew', for example, he describes how a dewdrop 'recollecting its own Light/ Does, in its pure and circling thoughts express/ The greater Heaven in a heaven less.'

The English Renaissance arguably began with Malory's re-telling of Arthurian legend in the *Morte Darthur* (see box page 16). John Milton, who brought the period to a close, had intended to write his own epic based on the story of King Arthur. However, he abandoned the project and took instead the subject of the fall of man in the Garden of Eden. Milton was not a churchman (although he was heavily involved in theological politics from the English Civil War in the 1640s and during the Commonwealth), but he was to write the greatest religious poem in English, *Paradise Lost.* By the time it was completed, Milton was already part of a past age, writing as he did with a Renaissance sensibility, rather than that of the Baroque.

Penshurst Place, Kent, the great hall, c.1340

Ben Jonson wrote a celebratory poem, 'To Penshurst' (see page 79) in praise of the seat of Robert Sidney, Viscount Lisle, in Kent. The great hall, shown here, dates from the end of the 14th century, and is typical of the dining halls of Renaissance houses and university colleges. Many of the great Elizabethan houses retained their medieval 'core', with modern extensions to provide better accommodation. The photograph looks from the high table past the central open hearth (lower right) to the screens passage, which connected the hall to the kitchens. The screens passage created a natural backdrop for dramatic performances (see page 23).

TIMELINE

Dates of plays are of first performance unless otherwise stated.
Dates of prose and poetry are of first publication unless otherwise stated.

Plays and theatrical history	Poetry and prose	History
	1475 Caxton's translation of *The Recuyell of the Historyes of Troye* first book to be printed in English	**1476** Caxton sets up printing press in Westminster
		1485 accession of Henry VII
		1492 Columbus sails to the Americas
		1494 Treaty of Tordesillas
		1497 Cabot's expedition to look for Northwest Passage
		1509 death of Henry VII; accession of Henry VIII; marriage of Henry and Catherine of Aragon
		1510 Colet founds St Paul's School in London
	1511 Erasmus *In Praise of Folly*	
	c.1513-18 More *History of King Richard III*	**1513** Balboa reaches the Pacific Ocean
	1516 More *Utopia*; Erasmus *The Education of a Christian Prince*	**1516** Birth of Princess Mary
		1517 Luther nails 95 theses to door of Castle Church in Wittenberg
		1521 Henry VIII given title 'Defender of the Faith'; Luther appears at Diet of Worms
	1525 Tyndale's translation into English of New Testament printed in Cologne	
	1528 Castiglione *Il Cortegiano (The Courtier)* published in Italy	
1530 Skelton *Magnificence* published	**1531** Elyot *The Book named the Governor*	
		1533 Henry VIII marries Anne Boleyn; divorce of Henry VIII and Catherine of Aragon; birth of Princess Elizabeth
		1534 Act of Supremacy makes Henry VIII head of Church in England
	1535 Coverdale's translation into English of complete Bible published in Zurich	**1535** execution of Sir Thomas More
	1536 Machiavelli *The Prince* published in Italy	**1536** execution of Anne Boleyn; Henry marries Jane Seymour
		1536-9 Dissolution of the Monasteries

		1537 birth of Prince Edward and death of Jane Seymour
		1538 Henry VIII excommunicated from Catholic Church
	1539 Great Bible issued for use in English churches	**1539** marriage of Henry VIII and Anne of Cleves (annulled 1540)
		1540 Henry marries Catherine Howard
		1541 Jean Calvin founds Protestant Church in Geneva
		1542 execution of Catherine Howard
	1543 Copernicus *On the Revolutions of the Celestial Spheres*	**1543** marriage of Henry VIII and Katherine Parr
	1545 Ascham *Toxophilus*	
		1547 death of Henry VIII; accession of Edward VI
	1549 *Book of Common Prayer*	
c.1552 Udall *Ralph Roister Doister*		**1553** death of Edward VI; Lady Jane Grey on throne for nine days; accession of Mary
		1554 rebellion against Mary led by Sir Thomas Wyatt
		1558 death of Mary I; accession of Elizabeth I
		1559 Acts of Supremacy and Uniformity reestablish Church of England
1561 Sackville and Norton *Gorboduc/ Ferrex and Porrex*	**1561** Hoby *The Book of the Courtier*	
	1563 Foxe *The Book of Martyrs* published in English	
1567 first permanent stage erected at Red Lion, Whitechapel	**1568** Bishop's Bible	**1570** plague in London
	1570 Ascham *The Scholemaster*	
1576 Children of the Chapel Royal established; the Theatre opens		**1577-80** circumnavigation of the world by Sir Francis Drake
	1578 Lyly *Euphues, or the Anatomy of Wit*	
1583 Queen's Men established	**1579** North's translation of Plutarch's *Lives*; Spenser *The Shephearde's Calender*	**1586** legislation passed to restrict printing presses to London, Oxford and Cambridge
1587 Rose theatre opens; Marlowe *Tamburlaine the Great*		
c.1589 Kyd *The Spanish Tragedy*; Marlowe *The Massacre at Paris, Dr Faustus*	**1589** Hakluyt *Principal Navigations, Voyages and Discoveries of the English Nation* (revised 1598)	**1588** defeat of the Spanish Armada

83

Plays and theatrical history	Poetry and prose	History
1590 Marprelate controversy **c.1590** Marlowe *The Jew of Malta*; Shakespeare *Titus Andronicus* **1592** Rose theatre renovated and enlarged; Marlowe *Edward II* **1592-4** London theatres closed because of the plague **c.1593** Shakespeare *The Comedy of Errors* **c.1595** Shakespeare *Richard II, Romeo and Juliet* **1596** Swan theatre opens **c.1596** Shakespeare *A Midsummer Night's Dream* **1597** Nashe *The Isle of Dogs* **c.1597** Shakespeare *Henry IV, The Merry Wives of Windsor* **1598** Jonson *Every Man in his Humour* **c.1598** Shakespeare *Much Ado about Nothing* **1599** Globe theatre opens; Jonson *Every Man Out of his Humour*; Dekker *The Shoemaker's Holiday*; Shakespeare *Julius Caesar* **c.1599** Shakespeare *Henry V, As You Like It* **1600** Fortune theatre opens; Shakespeare *Hamlet* **c.1600** Shakespeare *Twelfth Night* **1603** Chamberlain's Men renamed the King's Men; Admiral's Men renamed Prince Henry's Men; Jonson *Sejanus*	**1590** Spenser *Faerie Queene* (Bks I-III) **1591** Sidney *Astrophil and Stella*; Raleigh *Report of the Fight about the Azores* **1593** Sidney *The Countess of Pembroke's Arcadia*; Shakespeare *Venus and Adonis* **1594** Hooker *Laws of Ecclesiastical Polity* (Bks I-IV); Shakespeare *The Rape of Lucrece*; Nashe *The Unfortunate Traveller* **1595** Sidney *The Defence of Poesy*; Spenser *Amoretti* and *Epithalamion* **1596** Spenser *Faerie Queene* (Bks IV-VI), *Prothalamion*; Raleigh *The Discovery of the Large, Rich and Beautiful Empire of Guiana* **1597** Hooker *Laws of Ecclesiastical Polity* (Bk V); **1598** Marlowe *Hero and Leander*	**1592-4** plague in London **1596** raid on Cadiz led by Earl of Essex **1598** rebellion in Ireland led by Earl of Tyrone **1601** rebellion and execution of Earl of Essex **1603** death of Elizabeth I; accession of James I of England and VI of Scotland; plague in London

c.1604 Shakespeare
Measure for Measure
1605 Jonson *Volpone*;
Jonson, Chapman and
Marston *Eastward Ho!*
c.1605 Shakespeare
King Lear
1606 Rose theatre
demolished
c.1607 Shakespeare *Antony and Cleopatra*
1608 King's Men move into
Blackfriars theatre
c.1608 Shakespeare
Coriolanus, *Pericles*
1610 Jonson *The Alchemist*
c.1610 Shakespeare
Cymbeline
1611 Jonson *Catiline*
c.1611 Shakespeare *The Winter's Tale*, *The Tempest*
1613 Globe theatre burns
down; Webster *Duchess of Malfi*
1614 Hope theatre opens;
1616 Cockpit theatre opens;
Jonson *The Devil is an Ass*;
Jonson publishes complete
Works
1621 Fortune theatre
burns down; Middleton
Women Beware Women
1622 Middleton and Rowley
The Changeling
1623 First Folio edition of
Shakespeare's plays
1624 Middleton *A Game at Chess*

1633 Ford *'Tis Pity She's a Whore* printed

1642 Parliament closes
down all theatres

1605 Cervantes *Don Quixote*

1609 Shakespeare *Sonnets*

1611 Authorised Version of
the Bible; Coryat *Coryate's Crudities*

1621 Burton *The Anatomy of Melancholy*

1624 Donne *Devotions upon Emergent Occasions*
1628 Harvey *An Anatomical Exercise Concerning the Motion of the Heart and Blood in Animals*
1633 Donne *Songs and Sonets*; Herbert *The Temple*
1640 English edition of
Machiavelli's *The Prince* published
1648 Herrick *Hesperides and Noble Numbers*

1667 Milton *Paradise Lost*

1605 The Gunpowder Plot

1607 English colony founded
in Virginia

1609 plague in London

1620 Pilgrim Fathers sail
from Plymouth to the 'New World'

1625 death of James I;
accession of Charles I
1629 Parliament dissolved

1642-8 English Civil War
1649 execution of Charles I;
declaration of the
Commonwealth

1660 restoration of the
monarchy

8 5

GLOSSARY OF TERMS

allegory/ical a story or painting in which there is a second meaning beyond the literal or primary meaning. Allegory is often used to communicate religious, political or other abstract ideas in a way designed to bring out correspondences between the literal and the non-literal levels.

Arcadia a region of Ancient Greece, used as the setting for events and people in *pastoral* writing. Populated by shepherds and nymphs, Arcadia symbolized a rural existence free from commercial or cosmopolitan values during the mythical 'Golden Age'.

blank verse poetry written in *iambic pentameter* without rhyme. Used for the first time by Henry Howard, Earl of Surrey in his translation of Virgil's *Aeneid*, and first used in drama by Christopher Marlowe. Shakespeare and other playwrights used blank verse widely, as the verse form imitates most closely the natural speech rhythms of English.

broadsheet/broadside ballad a cheap form of publishing songs and poetry often based on topical issues and current affairs and sold in public places. Broadsheets were printed on one side only, and often illustrated with woodcut engravings.

Calvinism/ist the teachings and beliefs of Jean Calvin, the French Protestant reformer. Calvinism included a belief in predestination – the idea that a person's soul is selected for heaven or damnation before that person has been born.

Church of England the Christian church established by Henry VIII and developed in the reigns of Edward VI and Elizabeth I. It was a reformed (Protestant) church that preserved aspects of Catholicism while replacing the supreme authority of the pope with that of the monarch.

citizen comedy/city comedy comedies written in the first half of the 17th century, set in contemporary London and concerned with the activities of the middle class. The best-known examples include Thomas Dekker's *The Shoemaker's Holiday,* Ben Jonson's *Bartholomew Fair* and Thomas Middleton's *A Chaste Maid in Cheapside*.

comedy of humours a form of *satirical* comedy developed by George Chapman and Ben Jonson in which characters are tricked into losing their money, social respect and status as a result of their own greed and egotism. Jonson took the doctrine of the *humours* as his starting point (see page 10).

didactic a work of art or piece of writing intended to teach or instruct its audience in a moral or physical way. Medieval literature in particular was strongly didactic, supporting the beliefs of the Roman Catholic church.

Dissolution of the Monasteries the destruction of the influence of the religious monastic houses during the reign of Henry VIII as a prelude to the English Reformation. On Henry's orders, Thomas Cromwell oversaw the demolition of abbeys, nunneries and monasteries, and their land and treasures were surrendered to the Crown.

eclogue originally, a sequence of *pastoral* poems by the Latin poet Virgil. In English poetry, a poem imitating Virgil's style or subject matter, and dealing with shepherds and rural life.

epigram a short, witty poem of a few lines usually *satirical* or complimentary in tone. In English poetry the form was developed by Ben Jonson, John Donne and Robert Herrick. The following is an example by Jonson:
'He that fears death, or mourns it in the just,
Shows of the resurrection little trust.'

essay A literary form created and named by the French writer Michel de Montaigne, and first adopted in English by Sir Francis Bacon. An essay is usually in prose and discusses a topic or a variety of topics in a relatively informal manner.

eulogy a speech praising the qualities and ability of someone, especially commemorating one who has died.

euphuism an elaborate and high-flown style of prose writing, named after *Euphues, the Anatomy of Wit* and its sequel *Euphues his England* (1580) by John Lyly. Euphuism is characterized by alliteration, balanced clauses, *rhetorical* questions and series of similes.

farce/ical a play or other dramatic work that is funny on a superficial level, and depends less upon words and language than upon character and situation. Repeated physical action, unlikely scenarios and exaggerated character and plot are all key ingredients.

folio a page made by folding a full-sized sheet of printer's paper once, or the name given to a book made up of paper folded in this way. As a result of the amount of paper used, a folio volume was the most expensive book available and thus was reserved for special publications.

foul papers the name given to the first rough draft of a play. The foul papers were used as the basis for the *prompt-book*.

genre a kind or class of writing. The term can be used to distinguish the basic categories of prose, poetry and drama, or to define different kinds of writing within those genres, such as *pastoral*, *satire*, epic or *lyric poetry*.

Gloriana one of the names used to celebrate Queen Elizabeth I by Edmund Spenser in his poem *The Faerie Queene*. The name was also widely used in other poetry and in *madrigals*.

guilds associations of people with common interests or work, formed during the medieval period to protect business interests, to maintain standards, and to look after their members. Guilds were closely linked to the Church.

Holy Roman Emperor the ruler of the Holy Roman Empire, which had its origins in the empire founded by the Frankish ruler Charlemagne in AD800 and which lasted until 1806. Charlemagne was crowned emperor of the Romans by Pope Leo III, and the Holy Roman Empire continued to be closely associated with the Roman Catholic Church.

Huguenots the name given to followers in France of the Protestant reformer Jean *Calvin*. Rivalry between the Huguenots and French Catholics led to the St Bartholomew's Day massacre in 1572, when thousands of Huguenots were killed.

humanism/ist a movement that flourished in Europe during the Renaissance which laid the emphasis on humans and human potential, in contrast to the medieval view of humans as essentially sinful beings. Humanists such as John Colet, Desiderius Erasmus and Sir Thomas More studied and wrote about the works of Classical Greek and Roman authors to deepen their understanding of human society. Humanism encouraged scholars to challenge the domination of the Catholic Church, which for centuries had dictated the direction of philosophy and art in Europe.

humours the belief – originating with the ancient Greeks – that the human body was made up of four liquids, or humours: black bile, phlegm, blood and yellow bile. Ideally, the four humours were equally balanced in the body, but a person's character was thought to be the result of the predominance of one or more humours.

iambic pentameter a line of poetry composed of five regular rhythmical units (or iambs) in which the second syllable of each unit carries more weight than the first. For example, "So *foul* and *fair a day* I *have* not *seen*" (*Macbeth*). Iambic pentameter is the commonest rhythmic pattern in English verse; it can be rhymed, or used in the form of **blank verse**.

iconography in art, the use of an image to represent something beyond its surface meaning.

liturgy the approved form of worship in a Christian church service, particularly relating to Holy Communion. The forms of all services are contained in the *Book of Common Prayer*.

lyric poetry originally, poetry intended to be accompanied on the lyre. In the Renaissance, poetry divided into stanzas with a song-like quality, and often concerned with love and similar emotions.

madrigal a musical setting of secular *lyric poetry* for unaccompanied voices singing in parts.

masque a spectacular performance characterized by elaborate costumes, formal dancing and music, and sophisticated stage scenery and machinery. The playwright Ben Jonson and designer Inigo Jones collaborated to produce some of the most famous masques between 1605 and 1631, staged at court and in the great country houses of the aristocracy.

Middle Ages the term for the period of history in Europe between the fall of the Roman Empire (5th century AD) and the start of the Renaissance (14th century).

morality play a modern term used to describe plays, usually anonymous, written from the 15th century to the mid-16th century. Unlike *mystery plays*, morality plays are not based on Biblical scenes, but instead dramatize social and moral issues in an **allegorical** context.

mumming (mummers' plays) mumming plays all involved the same basic plot in which St George fights an infidel knight; one of the warriors is killed but is brought back to life by a doctor. Mumming plays included dumbshow and masks, and were related to Italian masquerade.

mystery plays medieval dramas based on Bible stories and performed on major Church holy days (Christmas, Easter, Pentecost and Corpus Christi). They were performed outside, on large carts or pageants, by local town **guilds**.

octave in the Italian ('Petrarchan') form of the **sonnet**, the first stanza of eight lines, with a rhyme scheme of *abba abba*.

oratory the art of public speaking.

pamphlet a short work, published with soft covers. In the Renaissance, pamphlets were often argumentative, written to attack or defend a person or issue. Pamphlets were the forerunner of journalism.

pastoral a form of literature celebrating the innocent lives of shepherds and shepherdesses in an idealized rural setting, often known as **Arcadia**. The pastoral tradition started with Classical authors such as the Greek poet Theocritus and the Latin poet Virgil, and was revived in the Renaissance period by writers such as Edmund Spenser and Sir Philip Sidney.

picaresque originally a story that told the exploits of a servant (from the Spanish *picaró*) who enjoys a series of escapades in the service of several masters. It came to mean a story made up of several largely unrelated episodes held together by the presence of a central character.

plantations/planters the term used to describe the colonization of Ireland and, later, America by English and, in Ulster, Scottish settlers from 1556 onwards. These settlers were known as planters.

Presbyterian/ism one of the reformed churches established by Jean Calvin in Switzerland and John Knox in Scotland in the 16th century. The term comes from *presbyter*, a Greek word meaning 'elder'. Presbyterianism is a system of church organization in which congregations are governed by boards of elders, rather than by bishops appointed by the Crown.

prompt-book the copy of a play used by a theatrical company to prepare for its production. It was transcribed from the *foul papers*, and it was the manuscript from which individual parts were copied.

Protestant/ism a general term that describes any of the churches that broke away from the Roman Catholic Church during or after the Reformation. It comes from the Latin *protestans* meaning 'one who protests'.

Puritan/ism a term that describes those English Protestant reformers who rejected the moderate stance taken by Queen Elizabeth I on religious matters, and who thought that the Church of England should go further in its reforms. It included groups such as the *Presbyterians*.

quarto a page made by folding a full-sized sheet of printer's paper twice, or the name given to a book made up of paper folded in this way. Quarto volumes used less paper than *folio* volumes and were therefore cheaper. Individual plays were usually printed in this format.

quatrain a group of four lines of poetry, bound together by their rhyme scheme. In an English or Shakespearean *sonnet*, the 14 lines are arranged into three quatrains and a final rhyming couplet.

Reformation the term used to describe the large-scale protest against the Roman Catholic Church that started in the 16th century, and which led to the development of the *Protestant* churches. Many people consider that the Reformation started when Martin Luther nailed his 95 theses to the door of a church in Wittenberg (1517).

revenge tragedy a particular form of tragedy which concerns itself with a character's task of revenging a wrong committed against him or his family (such characters are usually male). Madness, ghosts, rape, poison and murder are standard ingredients of revenge tragedy; the best-known examples in Renaissance drama are Kyd's *The Spanish Tragedy*, Shakespeare's *Hamlet* and *The Revenger's Tragedy* (1607), traditionally attributed to Cyril Tourneur but now regarded as the work of Thomas Middleton.

rhetoric/al a style of speech or writing intended to persuade its audience through its power and elegance. Often employing specific formal techniques, rhetoric was a Classical skill admired and imitated by medieval and Renaissance writers.

satire/ical a type of writing that uses mockery, particularly through exaggeration or irony, to expose the moral failings and deficiencies of individual public figures or of society at large.

sestet in the Italian ('Petrarchan') form of the *sonnet*, the second stanza of six lines, with a rhyme scheme of usually either *cdcdcd* or *cdecde*.

sonnet a poem consisting of 14 lines of equal length, arranged according to one of a variety of rhyme schemes.

sprezzatura in *The Book of the Courtier* by the Italian humanist Baldassare Castiglione, *sprezzatura* is defined as an effortless ability, translated by Sir Thomas Hoby as 'simplicity or recklessness'.

tiring house the backstage area of a theatre.

vernacular the language of a particular people or place; in the context of the translation of the Bible and liturgy, the term refers to the language that allowed people greater understanding of Scripture.

volta an Italian word meaning 'turn', used to describe the moment at which the thought pattern in a *sonnet* changes direction, between the *octave* and the *sestet*.

BIOGRAPHICAL GLOSSARY

Bacon, Sir Francis (1561-1626) writer and philosopher. Born in York House, London, he was educated at Cambridge. He became a lawyer and then in 1584 was elected to Parliament. From 1591, he enjoyed the patronage of the Earl of Essex, favorite of Queen Elizabeth, but when Essex led a revolt against the queen ten years later, Bacon was instrumental in ensuring that his former patron was convicted. Bacon rose to power during the reign of James I, becoming Solicitor-General in 1607, Attorney-General in 1613, Lord Keeper in 1617 and Lord Chancellor in 1618. However, he had many rivals, most notably Sir Edward Coke, who, in 1621, accused Bacon of corruption. When Bacon admitted his guilt, he was dismissed from office, fined, and imprisoned briefly in the Tower of London. His public life over, he spent the rest of his life studying and writing. He was the first English writer to adopt the essay as a literary form, but his most influential works were *The Advancement of Learning* (1605) and *Novum Organum* (1620), both of which were concerned with the use of knowledge to improve human understanding of the natural world. He died after catching a chill while studying snow.

Caxton, William (c.1422-c.91) printer and translator. Born in Kent, he became a cloth merchant and moved to Bruges in Belgium in 1441. He probably learned how to print in Cologne in 1471-2. He printed the first book in English, his own translation of *The Recuyell of the Historyes of Troye*, in Bruges in 1475. In 1476 he returned to England and set up a wooden printing press in Westminster. In the course of the next 15 years he printed about 100 books including Geoffrey Chaucer's *The Canterbury Tales* and Sir Thomas Malory's *Morte Darthur*.

Colet, John (c.1467-1519) scholar and humanist. Born in London, he went to Oxford University before travelling and studying in France and Italy for three years. From 1496-1504 he lectured on the Bible at Oxford, where Erasmus was among his audience. He became a friend of Erasmus and of Sir Thomas More. In 1504 Colet became Dean of St Paul's Cathedral and in 1509-10 founded St Paul's School. Colet was a humanist, influenced by Plato, and not afraid to speak out against religious practice when he felt it was driven not by a recognition of humanity's needs but by the Church's own ends.

Dekker, Thomas (c.1570-1632) playwright and pamphlet writer. Little is known about his early life, but it is likely that he was born and brought up in London, as much of his writing vividly describes life in the city. In about 1595 he was commissioned by the theatre manager Philip Henslowe to write plays, often in collaboration with other playwrights such as Webster and Middleton. Despite this work, Dekker fell into debt and was imprisoned briefly in 1598-9 and for six years from 1613-19. Dekker had a hand in about 50 plays, the best-known being *The Shoemaker's Holiday* (1599) and *The Roaring Girl* (1610). His pamphlets often describe life in London: *The Wonderfull Yeare,* for example, (1603) which charts the progress of the plague in the city.

Donne, John (1572-1631) poet and cleric. Born in London, and brought up in the Roman Catholic faith, he studied at Oxford and at Cambridge, but his faith prevented him from taking a degree (he would have been obliged to swear the oath of allegiance to the Protestant queen, Elizabeth). He became a law student at Lincoln's Inn in 1594. Four years later he sailed with the Earl of Essex to sack Cadiz. The following year, he went to the Azores to hunt Spanish treasure ships with a fleet commanded by Sir Walter Raleigh. On his return from this expedition, Donne became secretary to Sir Thomas Egerton, Lord Keeper of the Great Seal. It is likely that by this time he had become an Anglican. It was in the Egerton household that Donne met and fell in love with Ann More, niece of Lady Egerton. Knowing that their match would not meet with approval, the two married secretly in 1601. When the marriage was discovered, Donne was dismissed from his post and briefly imprisoned. The disgraced couple lived in poverty for many years while Donne tried to find a patron and employment. They had 12 children, seven of whom survived, but Ann herself died after the birth of the twelfth child in 1617. Two years earlier, Donne had been ordained a priest in the Church of England and was appointed a royal chaplain. He soon established a reputation as a fine preacher, becoming a favorite of James I, and in 1621 he was appointed Dean of St Paul's Cathedral. In 1623 Donne fell ill and during this sickness wrote *Devotions upon Emergent Occasions*, published a year later. After King James's death, Donne preached his first sermon to the new king, Charles I, in 1625. He was also to preach his last sermon before the king, in 1631, which was published shortly afterwards as '*Death's Duel*'. Donne was one of the leading 'Metaphysical' poets, and his writing is characterized above all by wit, in the sense of an ingenious use of language.

Harvey, William (1578-1657) physician. Born in Kent, he was educated at the King's School in Canterbury and at Cambridge University. He then went to the University of Padua in Italy to continue his medical training. It was here that he began his experiments and investigations into the circulation of the blood. Harvey returned to England in 1602 and soon after married Elizabeth Browne, daughter of the king's physician. Harvey became physician at St Bartholomew's Hospital in London, a position he held for 34 years. He was also physician to many distinguished people, including Sir Francis Bacon, and, after 1618, to King James and subsequently King Charles I. Harvey published his theories on the circulation of the blood and the function of the heart in 1628, causing much controversy.

Herbert, George (1593-1633) poet. Born into a noble family, he went to Westminster School in London and Cambridge University, where he was an outstanding scholar and appointed University Orator. Herbert's mother, Lady Magdalene Herbert, was a patron of John Donne, and Herbert counted both Donne and Francis Bacon among his friends. In 1629 he married Jane Danvers, and they adopted two of Herbert's orphaned nieces. In 1630 Herbert became a priest, working at Bemerton in Wiltshire. However, by 1633 he realized he was dying. He sent his poems to another friend, Nicolas Ferrar, asking for his opinion about publishing them. They appeared in 1633, after Herbert's death, to great admiration, in a volume called *The Temple*.

Howard, Henry (Earl of Surrey) (1517-47) poet. Eldest son of Sir Thomas Howard, he took the title of Earl of Surrey when his father became 3rd Duke of Norfolk in 1524. From 1530-2 he lived at Windsor where he was companion to Henry Fitzroy, the illegitimate son of Henry VIII. There was talk of his being a suitor to Henry's eldest daughter, Mary, but in 1532 he married Lady Frances de Vere, daughter of the Earl of Oxford. Surrey's favor at court began to decline after Henry VIII married Jane Seymour: the Seymours plotted against the Howards, accusing Surrey of helping Roman Catholics in a rebellion. For this Surrey was confined to Windsor from 1537-9. It was during this time that he probably wrote much of the poetry for which he is remembered. Surrey once again came into favour after his cousin, Catherine Howard, married King Henry, and he fought in various campaigns in Scotland and France. However, in 1546, when it was clear that the old king was dying, enmity between the Howards and the Seymours flared up once more. Surrey and his father were both arrested for treason, and Surrey was executed on Tower Hill. His father was saved only because Henry VIII died before the death sentence could be carried out.

Jonson, Ben(jamin) (1572-1637) playwright and poet. Probably born in London, he went to Westminster School. He worked in his stepfather's trade, bricklaying, before serving as a soldier in Flanders. He then joined the Earl of Pembroke's Men, and was one of the actors imprisoned for

writing and performing *The Isle of Dogs* in 1597 (see page 42). By this time he was also working for the theatrical manager Philip Henslowe as an actor and playwright. He had his first major success in 1598 with *Every Man in his Humour*. The same year he killed a fellow actor, Gabriel Spenser, in a duel, for which he escaped execution only by pleading 'benefit of clergy' (the ability to read from the Latin Bible). He was, however, branded as a felon. Jonson hoped to cash in on the success of his previous work with its follow-up, *Every Man Out of his Humour* (1599), but the play was a disaster. Jonson had to find another company for which to write, and he turned to one of the children's companies for which he wrote *Cynthia's Revels* (1600) and *Poetaster* (1601). His first tragedy, *Sejanus,* was performed at the Globe in 1603 and landed Jonson in trouble because of its subject matter – conspiracies at court. The following year, Jonson was imprisoned once more for his part in another controversial play *Eastward Ho!* (1605) (see page 46). Despite these brushes with authority, Jonson presented his first court masque, *The Masque of Blackness*, in 1605, the first of many collaborations with the designer Inigo Jones. The following years saw the performance of Jonson's greatest works, including *Volpone* (1605), *Epicoene: or, The Silent Woman* (1609), *The Alchemist* (1610) and *Bartholomew Fair* (1614). In 1616 he published a folio edition of his own works; in the same year he was given a royal pension. From 1618-19, he undertook a walking tour from London to Scotland, where he visited the Scots poet William Drummond of Hawthornden, and in 1619 he was made an Honorary Master of Arts by Oxford University. In 1628 Jonson suffered a stroke and was confined to his bed until his death in 1637.

Marlowe, Christopher (1564-93) poet and playwright. Born in Canterbury, he was the son of a well-established shoemaker. He attended the King's School in Canterbury from the age of 15, and from there went to Cambridge University. He graduated with a BA in 1584 and remained in Cambridge for three more years to study for his MA degree. However, the university was uncertain whether to grant him his MA since he had frequently been absent from his studies; the government intervened on his behalf, declaring that he had been employed 'on matters touching the benefit of his country', which has led to the belief that he was employed in Elizabeth's secret service as a messenger or spy. After Cambridge he moved to London, where he quickly became involved in theatrical life. He had his first success in 1587 with *Tamburlaine the Great*. During that time he was a

FURTHER READING

Chapter 1 An Age of Discovery

Briggs, Julia. *This Stage-Play World,* 2nd edition. New York: Oxford University Press, 1997. A wide-ranging study of Renaissance culture.

Ford, Boris, ed. *The New Pelican Guide to English Literature, Volume 2: The Age of Shakespeare.* London: Penguin, 1982. Detailed chapters on individual authors, music and the theatre.

————. *The New Pelican Guide to English Literature, Volume 3: From Donne to Marvell.* London: Penguin, 1982. Provides information on the historical and social context of the period up to Restoration, as well as studies of individual authors.

Kinney, Arthur F., ed. *The Cambridge Companion to English Literature 1500–1600.* New York: Cambridge University Press, 2000.

MacCulloch, Diarmaid. *Tudor Church Militant: Edward VI and the Protestant Reformation.* London: Penguin, 1999.

Roston, Murray. *Sixteenth-Century English Literature.* New York: Schocken Books, 1982.

Strong, Roy. *The Cult of Elizabeth.* 1977. Reprint, Berkeley: University of California Press, 1987.

Wynne-Davies, Marion, ed. *Bloomsbury Guides to English Literature: The Renaissance.* London: Bloomsbury, 1992. A useful A-Z guide, with four critical essays on Renaissance literature.

Chapters 2 and 3 Drama and the Shakespearean Theatre

Blakemore Evans, G. ed. *Elizabethan-Jacobean Drama: The Theatre in Its Time.* Chicago: New Amsterdam Books, 1988. An anthology of contemporary writing on a range of themes related to Renaissance drama.

Braunmiller, A. R., and Michael Hattaway, eds. *The Cambridge Companion to English Renaissance Drama.* New York: Cambridge University Press, 1990.

Gibbons, Brian. *Jacobean City Comedy*, 2nd edition. London: Routledge, 1980.

Gurr, Andrew. *Playgoing in Shakespeare's London.* Cambridge, England: Cambridge University Press, 1987.

————. *The Shakespearean Stage 1574–1642.* Cambridge, England: Cambridge University Press, 1992. These two books by Andrew Gurr are highly informative and well organized. The relationships among the theatre companies and the development of theatres in London are clearly explained.

Happé, Peter. *English Drama Before Shakespeare.* London: Longman, 1999.

Leggatt, Alexander. *English Drama: Shakespeare to the Restoration, 1590–1660.* London: Longman, 1988.

Orgel, Stephen. *The Jonsonian Masque.* 1965. Reprint, New York: Columbia University Press, 1981.

Thomson, Peter. *Shakespeare's Professional Career.* New York: Cambridge University Press, 1992. A well-illustrated account of Shakespeare's life in the theatre, offering a good sense of the social context.

Wells, Stanley, ed. *The Cambridge Companion to Shakespeare Studies.* New York: Cambridge University Press, 1986.

Wells, Stanley, and Margreta de Grazia, eds. *The Cambridge Companion to Shakespeare.* New York: Cambridge University Press, 2001. Both Cambridge Companions offer essays on topics reflecting current critical thinking on Shakespeare and the drama of his time.

Chapter 4 Prose

Lewis, C. S. *Oxford History of English Literature, Volume IV: Poetry and Prose in the 16th Century.* 1954. Reprint, New York: Oxford University Press, 1990.

Pooley, Roger. *English Prose of the 17th Century.* London: Longman, 1992.

Ricks, Christopher, ed. *English Poetry and Prose 1540–1674.* 1981. Reprint, New York: Viking Penguin, 1994. Concentrates on poets of the period but includes a substantial chapter on Renaissance prose by John Carey.

Chapter 5 Poetry

Carey, John. *John Donne: Life, Mind and Art.* 1981. Reprint, London: Faber & Faber, 1991. A critical biography that links the preoccupations in Donne's poetry to his background and upbringing.

Corns, Thomas N., ed. *The Cambridge Companion to English Poetry: Donne to Marvell.* New York: Cambridge University Press, 1993.

Heale, Elizabeth. *Wyatt, Surrey and Early Tudor Poetry.* London: Longman, 1998.

Leggatt, Alexander. *Ben Jonson: His Vision and His Art.* New York: Routledge, 1981. Looks at Jonson's poetry as well as drama and masques.

Norbrook, David. *Poetry and Politics in the English Renaissance.* New York: Routledge, 1984.

Waller, Gary. *English Poetry of the 16th Century.* London: Longman, 1993.

Websites

The following websites are excellent gateways for further research in Renaissance literature, providing access to hundreds of useful sites:

http://www.luminarium.org/renlit/renaissanceinfo.htm

http://www.english.cam.ac.uk/ceres/links.htm

http://newark.rutgers.edu/~jlynch/Lit/ren.htm

INDEX